SPORTING SUPERMEN

SPORTING SUPERMEN

The True Stories of Our Childhood Comic Heroes

Brendan Gallagher

Aurum

First published in Great Britain
2006 by Aurum Press Ltd
25 Bedford Avenue, London WC1B 3AT
www.aurumpress.co.uk

CONTENTS

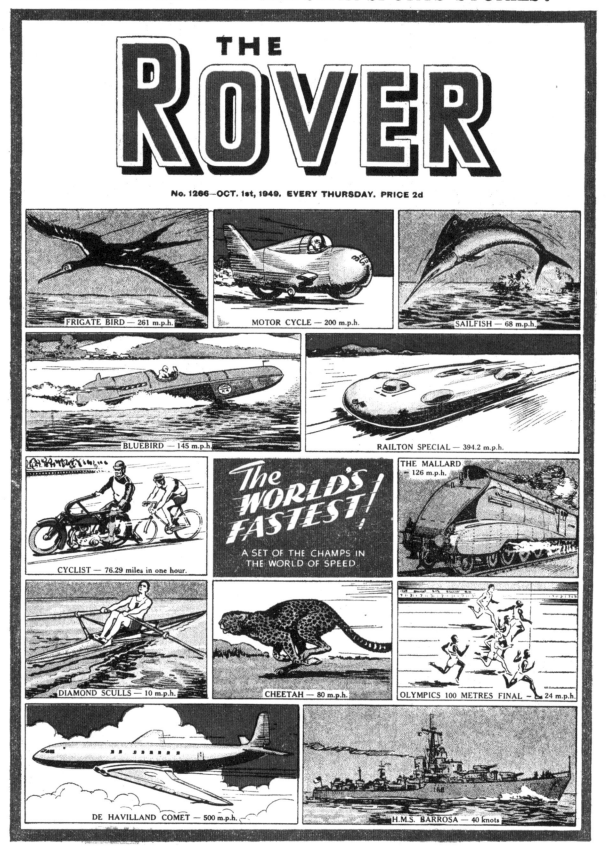

INTRODUCTION

Perhaps the 'maturity' of middle age – though the two are often mutually exclusive in the profession of sport journalism – imposes a retrospective feel-good factor onto memories of one's earlier years, lending them an air of enchantment that didn't actually exist at the time. But when it comes to comic book heroes – and comic book *sporting* heroes in particular – you would always be right to trust your memory. To this day I can think of very few pleasures that compare with the barely suppressed weekly excitement I felt in early adolescence when I heard the paper boy pushing my comic, or comics, of choice through the letter box every Tuesday morning, landing solidly on the mat with a satisfying thud.

I would be out of sight in the kitchen, ears pricked, primed for their arrival. Time was always tight. Breakfast – full Irish in our household – was still only half finished and there was my rugby kit to find and pack for an after school training session that night. And my priceless Surrey County Council schools' bus pass – gold dust in a household where money was tight – had gone missing again. As usual, it was to be found down the side of the settee. There were also early morning chores to complete, my contribution to the Gallagher household – namely stoking up the coal-fired boiler and loading the coal scuttle from the bunker outside; grubby work which, theoretically, was to be completed *before* donning my school uniform. Time was very tight indeed. It was 7 a.m. and the 424 bus to Reigate went at 7.21 a.m. from the triangle some five minutes walk away – to miss it and be late for school always resulted in a detention.

The pressure was mounting, but despite everything there was always time to race to the door, recklessly discard the daily newspapers, and eagerly flick through the comics – mine were *Victor*, *Tiger*, occasionally *Valiant* and, briefly, *Scorcher* – scanning them with the practiced eye of a veteran lawyer revising his brief. They could be read and reread at leisure later that night but the immediate priority was to quickly check the outcome of last week's cliffhanger and digest a brief synopsis of the new storylines. That way you could deliciously anticipate the evening that lay ahead. The entire process took barely a minute but it seemed infinitely longer, a rare opportunity for 'me time' in a schoolboy world which it seemed was spent following the instructions and wishes of others.

Reading the comics on the bus ride to school was not an option. They were a private pleasure and not, under any circumstances, to be shared with others on a noisy and overcrowded bus. They constituted my own fantasy dream world. A non-narcotic, highly addictive chill pill. After I'd thoroughly consumed them, they were carefully collated and stored, prized items to be treasured. Certainly I don't remember seeing my friends and fellow travellers – who I know to have been comic fiends – reading *their* favourites on the bus and nobody ever swapped their comics. They were too highly praised.

Joy was also unfettered on Christmas Eve when peering under the tree at your A4-shaped presents wrapped in paper through which (if held up to the light) it was just possible to make out the words *Victor Annual* or *Tiger Annual*. Agonizingly there were still another twenty-four hours to wait until you were allowed to open them, always after the Queen's speech on TV on Christmas Day. And even then dad or some bloody uncle or older cousin would pluck your annual from your grasp and read it from cover to cover before dismissively tossing it back in your direction. Fancy anybody wanting to read that rubbish, was the baffling unspoken rebuke. Adults can be very strange.

So, come Yuletide, you waited patiently. And eventually, in the dog days between Christmas and New Year, when the grown-ups were bored and it was lashing with rain, you settled down for a couple of hours of intensive fireside reading. The Christmas annuals seemed that much bigger and better, the stories even more spectacular and heroic. They renewed your faith and enthusiasm for the weekly comics that kept you amused all year.

Little did we know that those much cherished Christmas annuals often featured comic strips that had appeared decades earlier, the publishers assuming that each successive generation would move on and never revisit their youth. Roy of the Rovers had been going since the early fifties; and Alf Tupper was even earlier – the stories I had first read were simply rehashes of the original series that started in 1949. And why not? Nobody in their right mind would still be reading the stories so many years later, would they? Surely not! The concept of 'retro' clearly hadn't been invented yet . . .

But ignorance was bliss, so we tucked in with relish. It was a fantasy world, yes, but a world full of sporting heroes who seemed so authentic and plausible that fact and fiction merged seamlessly. Hundreds of top British sportsmen were

THE TRUTH ABOUT WILSON
Wilson in full flow was a sight to behold. Note the head tilted back in the manner of Britain's Olympic quarter-mile champion Eric Liddell, the hero of the film **Chariots of Fire**. *But who was copying whom?*

WILSON SOARS TO NEW HEIGHTS
Wilson won the pole vault during the Black Olympics of 1948, clearing a height of 20 feet. Bamboo poles that snapped provided the main opposition.

first inspired to follow their dreams by the comic book heroes they worshipped in their youth. I would also suggest – and educationalists may not like this – that the vast majority of young boys actually learned to read by devouring the comics.

One of the great attractions of the comic book, especially the illustrated text stories rather than the later comic strips, has to be the way in which they effortlessly sucked in all age groups. A nine- or ten-year-old could skim-read, understand and enjoy stories that were theoretically out of their league, while in so called 'mature middle age' you can still pick up the same story and read it without any embarrassment. Indeed, the pleasure of nosing around a second-hand bookshop, stumbling across one of the old comic book annuals and turning straight to your favourite character is almost the equal of those sublime memories of childhood.

My era, which spanned the late sixties and early seventies, was at the tail end of the golden age of comic book heroes, but two of the three all-time greats were mercifully still going strong – Alf Tupper, the 'Tough of the Track'; and Roy of the Rovers, the first footballing superhero. To my mind, the trinity is completed by the almost mythical Wilson of the *Wizard* who I stumbled across much later in life, although he actually began early in the Second World War and somehow I missed the repeats.

Occasionally, over the years, I had come across reference to Wilson and his extraordinary feats in a newspaper or magazine article but he seemed to belong to a different generation. Grandad, while sipping cold tea from a Tizer bottle during his lunch break as a plasterer, would occasionally come out with the line, 'Only the incredible Wilson could do that', when considering some outrageous sports story in the *Daily Mail*, which he bought religiously ('for the cricket') despite being a lifelong Labour supporter and voter. Simple mathematics now tells me that grandad must have been well into his thirties when Wilson first appeared on the scene – proof that it wasn't just schoolboys who read about him.

About ten years ago I picked up a slim volume entitled *The Truth About Wilson* in a second-hand bookshop in Lewes for £5.99. Alas, I only had coppers in my pocket and reluctantly had to place it back the shelf. Not a clever move. Today you would have to pay in excess of a hundred and thirty pounds to buy it on Ebay, not that I've seen one there for two years now. Nevertheless, my interest had been aroused again, and I dug even deeper when compiling a

TIGER AND JAG

7D

EVERY MONDAY

13th SEPTEMBER, 1969

SKID SOLO

LYING SECOND IN THE DRIVERS' WORLD CHAMPIONSHIP, SKID SOLO WAS HOPING TO IMPROVE HIS POSITION WITH A WIN IN THE ITALIAN GRAND PRIX AT MONZA. BUT DURING PRACTICE ON THE DAY BEFORE THE RACE...

THE WHEEL'S LOCKED SOLID!

EVEN SKID COULDN'T HOLD THE CAR ON THE TRACK...

I'M GETTING OUT OF HERE, FAST!

SKID LEAPED CLEAR— JUST AS HIS MECHANICS SANDY McGRATH AND SPARROW SMITH ARRIVED...

WHAT WENT WRONG, SKID?

I DON'T KNOW, SANDY ... BUT GET IT FIXED. WE'VE GOT TWELVE HOURS BEFORE THE RACE STARTS!

CONTINUED ON NEXT PAGE

Australia 10 cents; New Zealand 10 cents; South Africa 10 cents; Rhodesia 1/-; East Africa 1.00c; West Africa 1/-; Malaysia 40 cents; Malta 9d.

WILSON = TRAINER OF CHAMPIONS

IS THIS A DAGGER I SEE BEFORE ME?
At one stage Wilson was heavily into cycling, and his extraordinary endurance made him a natural for the sport. He did, however, encounter one or two 'local difficulties' with unsavoury characters along the road.

Christmas special on comic book heroes for the *Daily Telegraph*. Back copies of the *Wizard* are hard to find but the pursuit is worthwhile – once you start reading Wilson stories, you can't put them down

What is their appeal, and indeed the appeal of Alf Tupper, Roy of the Rovers and all the others that you may recall from your youth? Everybody has their favourites. There was Gorgeous Gus; Raven on the Wing; Billy's Boots; Nipper; Johnny Cougar, the wrestler; Skid Solo, the Formula One ace; Philip Driver, the golfer; Limpalong Leslie; Kenny Kangaroo; Lags XI, the all-prisoner football team; Football Family Robinson; Nightingale Nobs, another wrestler; the Mudtown Marvels; Mr Frozen Face, as befits one of the world's great motorcyclists; the Shining Fist, a boxer you wouldn't mess with; Tennis Tramp and Buster; Mini Maestros; Bernard Briggs; the Goals of Jimmy Grant; Tipped for the Top; the Hard Man; the Tough Game; Hotshot Hamish; Jack of United; Jimmy of City; Cannonball Craig; Peter the Cat; Lord Rumsey's Rovers. And so the list goes on.

It's hard to quantify, because we live in a different era with different values, but the best anthology comics were based almost entirely on glorifying the British Empire and our Commonwealth allies, and were incredibly patriotic. There are numerous examples – the Wolf of Kabul and his mate Chang, who pulverised enemies with a cricket bat up

THE TOUGH OF THE TORCH
Rarely was it enough for Alf to simply win a race: that was too straightforward. Normally he was required to perform a good deed for the day as well. On this famous occasion he rescued a steeplejack who had become trapped while working on a tower.

FOOTBALL FAMILY ROBINSON
*'Ma' Robinson ruled with a rod of iron at Thatchem United, the football team
consisting entirely of members of the Robinson family.*

on the north-west Frontier; the huge Canadian Red Indian wrestler Johnny Cougar; Wilson going down to Africa to win the 'Black Olympics' and prove that Britain is best and that the white man reigned supreme. Political correctness just didn't exist in those days. Our heroes were always beating the 'Yanks' and 'Johnny Foreigner'. Germans were always referred to as the 'sausage noshers', and so on.

As the Empire disappeared, in the sixties and seventies, sensibilities quickly changed and you just couldn't get away with that sort of language. However, it seems that patriotism is very much back on the agenda again and it's no longer frowned upon to cheer and shout and glorify your own country as long as you don't denigrate and abuse others while you're doing so.

The target readership was essentially 'Boy Scouts with attitude' – young men who would somehow make do, improvise, beat the odds, overcome whatever hardship they faced, rout the opposition and do it all essentially by fair means not foul – though there were those, like Tough of the Track, who sailed very close to the wind.

When the majority of comics disappeared in the eighties, a gap appeared in our sporting culture – to be filled, strangely, by a new breed of sporting stars, mainly footballers, whose lives and loves became real life comic book strips as played out in the tabloids and on reality TV. The huge downside is that, with much less stringent levels of censorship, we are exposed to the unsanitised versions.

Many sportsmen – the overwhelming majority, in fact – are still glamorous, chivalrous, fair-minded, enjoy the good things in life without attracting undue attention and are fantastic role models. Others, alas, are mean-spirited, selfish, arrogant, drunken, money-driven, solvent-abusing, wife-beating, cross-dressing, cigar-stubbing, drug cheats who glory in their infamy and scarcely deserved gains.

What comic books and their sporting heroes did was to

BILLY'S BOOTS
*Losing, and then finding, Billy's Boots was the basic
storyline underpinning the entire series. Suitably shod,
Billy Dane became a world-beater.*

sort the wheat from the chaff and act as an unofficial censor. There were always a couple of villains or 'bad 'uns' around but they were always routed and thoroughly discredited. Some even saw the error of their ways and repented. Real life, of course, isn't always like that. Good guys often come a distant last.

Although, almost by definition, our comic book sporting heroes had to win or take gold, it could be a pretty harsh and grimy road to success. Flick through old copies of *Rover*, *Victor*, *Hotspur*, and *Valiant* – they blazed a trail for *Tiger*, *Scorcher* and *Roy of the Rovers* – and you are quickly struck by how austere life was in post-war Britain. And how calamitous.

Ken Barry is all set to appear on America's top TV show, but there is one big snag—Nightingale is caged in a New York police cell!

Wilson of the *Wizard* was rushed out to Australia in one episode, when the entire England cricket team die in a plane crash; Raven on the Wing was a starving gypsy kid in rags who made good on the football field; Alf Tupper, Tough of the Track, was an orphan who slept on the floor of Ike Smith's welding garage and had to make do with bread and dripping for breakfast, though he famously dined a great deal on fish and chips too.

Nipper Lawrence, the world's fastest wing, came from the grimy gutter of a bombed-out industrial town, while poor old Skid Solo was left so horribly maimed and burned after crashing in his last Grand Prix that his face could no longer be viewed.

Not everybody has approved of a comic book approach to adolescence. As George Orwell wrote in an essay on boys' weeklies in *Horizon* magazine:

It is probable that many people who would consider themselves extremely sophisticated and 'advanced' are actually carrying through life an imaginative background which they acquired in childhood . . . If that is so, the twopenny weeklies are of the deepest importance. Here

is the stuff that is read somewhere between the ages of twelve and eighteen by a very large proportion, perhaps an actual majority, of English boys, including many who will never read anything else except newspapers . . . and there is being pumped into them the conviction that the major problems of our time do not exist, that there is nothing wrong with laissez-faire capitalism, that foreigners are unimportant comics and that the British empire is a sort of charity concern which will last for ever.

Computer games and the arrival of digital technology were the final straw for comics – along with the invention of mountain bikes. At least we can welcome the latter. The former stifle the imagination and leave generations of youngsters with below average reading abilities.

Memories of their halcyon day may be fading but comic book heroes never die; its only their readership who get older and, if anything, we grow more appreciative with age.

Brendan Gallagher
August 2006

ALF TUPPER AND NIGHTINGALE NOBBS
Nightingale Nobbs was not to be trifled with; the Tough of the Track wanted to win, but by fair means, not foul.

William Wilson – The Life and Times of a Legend

CAREER DETAILS AND PERSONAL BEST PERFORMANCES

William Wilson (Great Britain).

BORN Stayling, Yorks 1.11.1795: Farm labourer turned athlete. Self-educated. Lived on Ambleside, Cleveland, Highlands of Suthlerland and finally Axmoor.

100M: 9.0 secs (WR) Philadelphia Decathlon 1947.

440YDS: 44.0 secs (Indoor WR) Madison Square Gardens, New York 1938; 42.0 (WR) Great Britain Relay split in the German Medley Relays, Leipzig 1939.

880YDS: 1min 40secs (WR) Relay split in German Medley Relays, Leipzig 1939.

MILE: 3min 48secs, Stamford Bridge 1938. Also 4mins 2 secs in the Stayling Easter Mile (cross country) in 1814.

HIGH JUMP: 7ft 1in (WR) Bellevue International Meeting 1938.

LONG JUMP: 28ft (WR) Philadelphia Decathlon 1947.

POLE VAULT: 20ft (WR) Black Olympics, 1948.

JAVELIN: 284ft (WR) Challenge to Jasper Falby, 1821. Note also left-handed javelin throw of 260ft, Philadelphia Decathlon 1947.

DISCUS: 170ft Philadelphia Decathlon, 1947.

SHOT PUTT: 81ft 3in (WR), The London Challenge Series 1833. Note also 58ft 6in left-handed to win the Crystal Palace International meeting in 1954.

HAMMER: 250ft (WR) The London Challenge Series (1833).

THROWING THE CRICKET BALL: 200yd (WR), June 1953 following Stoneshire's win over Highshire.

MARATHON: 2hrs 20min (Athens Games 1938).

ULTRA MARATHON: Ran 200 miles from Thirsk to London in 26hrs 30min (1832).

OTHER CAREER HIGHLIGHTS:

1813: Lifting the Grieve Stone, Ambleside, Yorkshire.

1815: Ran 20 miles cross country in 2 hours to warn the Duke of Wellington of Napoleon's advance at Quatre Bras.

1816: Jumped the 26ft Ponzine Canal to rescue Prince Piedmonte in Venice.

1832: Defeated World Heavyweight Boxing Champion Jem Sprigg.

1846: Wilson completes the first ascent, in three minutes, of 'Wilson's climb' a notorious vertical rockface in Cumbria. He then descends in exactly one minute.

1869: First ascent of the Wesserhorn Mountain, Switzerland.

1896: Second in the Olympic marathon.

1938: Defeats Gypsy Danny Ronda, undisputed boxing champion, over 15 rounds.

1939: Second ascent of the Wesserhorn Mountain. Selected to lead Britain's ascent of Everest but postponed due to WW11.

1940: 24 confirmed kills while flying Spitfires in the Battle of Britain.

1946: Wilson repeats the 'Wilson climb' in three minutes, and descends in one, to prove that he is not Corporal Green but in fact the 'Amazing Wilson'.

1952: Olympic Modern Pentathlon Champion (Athens).

1953: Takes 20 Australian wickets while bowling Australia out twice in a day to win the Ashes for England. Fastest delivery timed at 120mph. Scored a century in 28 balls for Stoneshire against Ribbleshire, the fastest first-class century of modern times.

WILSON

THE MAKINGS OF A CHAMPION

Sometimes the life of William Wilson seems just too incredible for words. His heroics ranged from a vital but hitherto unknown part in the Battle of Waterloo, to a glorious finale in the 1950s when he won the Olympic gold medal in the Modern Pentathlon and then went on to play a crucial role in England's spectacular Ashes win over the Australians just a year later. Since then we have heard little about him, as he steadfastly resists the lures of pro-fessional sport and remains suspicious of the media and publicity.

There have been infrequent sightings on the skyline of remote Axmoor, where he appears to have settled, after nearly two centuries spent roaming the high moorlands of England and Scotland. A lean figure dressed in black is still occasionally spotted, chasing deer and foxes, seemingly just for fun – a man who is manifestly at ease with nature. And then? Nothing for months, as he disappears back into the mist. The paparazzi, attracted by the promise of the £500,000 reward on offer from the *Sun* and *Hello!* for exclusive pictures, still stake out the lonely moor, after the latest reported sighting by a local farmer or rambler. They should know better by now. Wilson will only be found when he chooses to reveal himself. It was ever thus.

The 'Amazing Wilson' – or 'Wilson of the *Wizard*', as he was known for many years – has long been shrouded in mystery. This mystique is largely of his own making and, even now, we are still discovering evidence of previously undisclosed feats. No doubt this will always be the case but, in the interests of posterity, we can delay no longer in chronicling the known feats of Britain's greatest ever sportsman and – some would argue – Britain's greatest ever son. Revealing the secrets of his physical and mental capabilities, or at least trying to gain some insight into them, can surely benefit us all

In undertaking such a task I humbly follow in the steps of two giants of British sports journalism – W.S.K. Webb (who became better known as Captain Webb after his distinguished service during the Second World War), and Reg Webster. Webb worked as athletics correspondent, and later sports editor, of the *Daily Clarion*, and both he and Webster, the *Clarion*'s cricket correspondent, breathlessly chronicled Wilson's career during those brief periods when he emerged into the public eye. Their notes and reports have proved invaluable. Frank Ducker, a stalwart of the British Athletic Association before and after the Second World War – and a witness to many of Wilson's world record-breaking athletics performances – has also been a reliable and enthusiastic source of anecdotes. Thanks also to Ray Vale, a promising athlete before the Second World War, who mangled his leg in a crash behind enemy lines. Vale was nursed back to health by one Squadron Leader Greene who, as we will learn, bore an uncanny resemblance to Wilson. And, finally, we have the invaluable writings of the man himself. Encouraged by Webb, whom he trusted implicitly, Wilson allowed certain facets of his life to be revealed using extracts from his diary, which were eagerly published by the *Clarion*. This exercise was, alas, discontinued after two serialisations, as Wilson became increasingly alarmed at the publicity and attention it generated.

Wilson's own highly personal account of his life commenced on the morning of 14 March 1813. The previous evening, on an outcrop in the remote heartland of Ambleside moor, he had hoisted the mighty Grieve Stone high above his head and in doing so had proved himself worthy of learning the secret of the elixir of life from his friend Matthew, a two-hundred-year-old hermit who lived in a hidden cave nearby. He was seventeen years old and it was the most momentous day of his young life. But we are getting ahead of ourselves! As Wilson himself always proclaimed when training fellow athletes, there are no short cuts. You have to begin at the beginning . . .

THE YOUNG WILSON

William Wilson was born at Lambton Farm on 1 November 1795 just outside the village of Stayling on the edge of bleak Ambleside moor in north Yorkshire, apparently the only son of a hard-working and thrifty tenant farmer. Life was extremely physically demanding for young Wilson, but he wanted for nothing and lived for the outdoors. By the age of seven he was spending ten hours a day scaring off birds from the cornfields and revelling in the fresh air and freedom.

Wilson was acute in his observations. From high on the moor he was struck by how often he heard the Stayling church bell ring out forlornly to signify the latest funeral in the village. Why did people die so young? Was death

THE TRUTH ABOUT WILSON

MATTHEW, THE-TWO-HUNDRED-YEAR-OLD HERMIT
The incredible Wilson story began when he stumbled upon the recluse in a cave on Ambleside Moor. Matthew had travelled Europe and the Middle East looking for the elixir of life, which he eventually found in Kurdistan.

inevitable? Couldn't life be prolonged? He further noted that no birdlife or animals drank from the village well, preferring to use a spring some distance up a neighbouring outcrop. Despite a great deal of ridicule, he decided to do likewise. The animals were alive and thriving, while the human inhabitants of Stayling were dying at an alarming rate.

He also pondered the power of the mind. 'There is a hidden strength somewhere,' he noted. 'The body doesn't want to see it but, if it is made to, it can do much more than it otherwise would. I must learn how to turn on this reserve strength when needed.' Not the usual musings of a boy not yet ten years of age. Nobody else appeared to share his fascination with the powers of the human body and, in that respect, he was already set apart and isolated from his peers.

There were, of course, other factors motivating him to become strong and independent. Wilson used to receive regular thrashings from Jasper Falby – the demented and cruel son of the local landowner Squire Falby – and his thuggish friends, who seemed to mete out the punishments just for fun. Wilson vowed to get even. He started to lift rocks to improve his strength and, by the age of eleven, was wrestling young bull calves in his father's courtyard. He believed he was making progress until one over-ambitious day he came a cropper when he decided to tackle the farm's stud bull. Wilson was tossed dismissively over a fence and was lucky to escape with his life. That humiliation only spurred the single-minded Wilson on. He would escape to the moor and live off the land, at one with nature.

He quickly took to such a life, catching rabbits and fish and supplementing his diet with nuts and berries. He shed all clothes save for a loincloth and trained his body to resist the cold. It took a while but before long he arrived at a state where 'the body created its own warmth'. Not so fanciful as you might think. London lawyer Lewis Gordon Pugh has achieved notoriety in recent years by swimming with impunity in Arctic and Antarctic waters. Tests have revealed that his body temperature rises by 1.5 degrees Celsius simply by *looking* at cold water. Mind over matter? Or an inexplicable physiological reaction? Take your pick. Wilson was unquestionably ahead of his time.

Wandering on a remote corner of the moor one day, he stumbled across Matthew, a two-hundred-year-old hermit. It was to be the seminal moment of his life. Matthew was born in 1612 in London, where his father was an apothecary at the Court of James I. After studying medicine at the feet of Orlando, the physician to Charles I, Matthew travelled extensively in France, Germany and Spain, specifically looking at ways of prolonging life. Eventually he raised sufficient funds to visit Constantinople and continued on to Kurdistan in search of the famed shepherd folk who lived there, some of whom reportedly lived to the astonishing age of two hundred. This he found to be entirely true. The secret of their longevity lay in a unique herbal potion that slowed the heart down from a norm of between seventy and eighty beats per minute to a mere thirty.

Matthew found that, as well as prolonging life, the elixir

HOISTING THE MIGHTY GRIEVE STONE

Before Matthew would consider passing on the elixir Wilson had to prove himself, which he did by training every day to become only the second person in history to lift the Grieve Stone high on Ambleside Moor.

also provided the potential for man to increase his physical capabilities, as he wrote:

> If you are going to increase the capacity of your lungs and muscles through training you must slow down your heart proportionately. Remember the valves of the heart are subjected to wear and tear all the time. Once worn out they cannot be replaced. Slow down the heart and it will last longer. The human body is capable of many feats. We rarely push it to the limit. I have reason to believe there is scarcely anything we cannot accomplish.

Again these musings on improving human performance seem strangely prophetic. Two of the greatest athletes of the late twentieth century, both of whom who pushed back the boundaries of their sports – Finland's Lasse Viren and Great Britain's Steve Ovett – possessed heartbeats in the low thirties.

Matthew had been troubled by the possession of such momentous knowledge. 'When I returned to civilization I was struck by the immense amount of cruelty and suffering that people inflicted upon each other and I decided it was not worthwhile helping ordinary people to live longer than nature intended. I kept the secret to myself and led a simple life in many lands.'

Having surreptitiously watched young Wilson train on the moor for some months, however, he felt he had finally found a worthy confidant. First, though, he set Wilson a challenge: if he could train himself by natural means to lift the Grieve Stone – thought to be in the region of four hundredweight – he would be given access to the secrets.

The Grieve Stone had only been lifted once before, in 1692, by the Long Grieve – an eight-foot giant who'd held it above his head for ten full seconds to satisfy all witnesses.

Minutes later he collapsed and died from the exertion. Throughout history there has been a very real concern about how the human body would react to being pushed to the extreme of its limits – the expression 'a spent force' attests to the fear that a person's very essence could be drained from them in the process. That fear persisted until at least the 1980s – only then were world-class female athletes gradually allowed to compete at distances longer than 800 metres.

Matthew revealed that, should anything happen to him, a list of the contents and means of preparation for the potion was safely hidden in an envelope, placed in his favourite copy of Virgil, which stood on a natural rock shelf at the back of the cave.

Wilson, having also been advised by Matthew that sleep is another underestimated way of strengthening and repairing the body, attempted to lift the Grieve Stone every day and, over a period of months, was able to hoist it level with his shoulders. He learned the correct grip and gradually sensed the balance of the rock. He also raced foxes across the moor and, after one particularly exhausting chase, experienced the first of many coma-like blackouts that were to be his body's almost trademark reaction to particularly strenuous exertion. They were always short-lived and today the concept of 'oxygen debt' is widely recognised as a common physiological reaction *in extremis*.

Wilson briefly returned to work on the family farm when his father fell ill and then died. Events took a strange turn at this juncture with the revelation that Wilson senior had somehow stashed away five thousand pounds – well in excess of two million pounds at today's rates – which he left to his son after making provision for his wife to live with a sister in Hull. This is highly unsatisfactory from a biographical point

HE QUICKLY TOOK TO SUCH A LIFE, CATCHING RABBITS AND FISH . . .

Wilson quickly took to a life on the moor, catching rabbits and fish and harvesting the berries and nuts that Matthew had pointed out to him. He wanted for nothing. He was entirely self-sufficient and gradually built his strength.

of view and remains an irritating anomaly. There was no indication, prior to his father's death, of any substantial amount of money in the family. One senses Wilson was a little embarrassed by his newly acquired wealth, and he made no mention of its origins. It didn't fit with the austere backdrop of his spartan life, but it did, however, free him enough financially to live whatever life he chose.

So we return to 13 March 1813. It's easy to imagine the determined young Wilson, having rested and slept all day, walking slowly but with great intent towards the Grieve Stone, contemplating the task ahead. He takes up the story:

> I gripped the stone harder than ever, bent both knees so that I dipped halfway to the ground, then straightened them with a mighty jerk thrusting upwards with both arms with all my strength. The Grieve Stone rose on high, I had positioned myself beneath it with my leg-work. I only had to hold it aloft rigidly for ten seconds and my self-allotted task would be complete. The strain was tremendous. I felt that my arms were being pushed down into my shoulders. Everything was swimming around me. I swayed and staggered to and fro until I had counted twenty – then, using my last remaining strength, I tossed the massive weight from me as I threw myself backwards to the ground. For nearly a minute I fought down the sensation that I was choking, and then my head cleared. I had qualified for the mysterious cordial which Matthew had promised me – the elixir which would enable me to live for hundreds of years – perhaps forever!

His excitement jumps off the page. The young Wilson was intoxicated by the promise of eternal life. That night he sprinted back to the cave, firstly to tell Matthew the news and then, as was the deal, to sip the elixir and to take possession of the recipe.

But tragedy had struck! In a cruel twist of fate, just as Wilson was revelling in his moment of triumph, his mentor had been killed in a rock fall. After pausing to write his first emotional diary entry the following morning, he set about removing the debris – nearly 100 tons of rubble – to find the copy of Virgil. One can only imagine the mental agony of this task, grieving for his friend and wondering every minute whether he was to be denied. So near and yet so far. The task took three whole months, working fourteen hours a day, but finally he had the secret of life in his hands.

> I jumped down with it, blew the dust from the cover and saw that it was the book I sought. It was Matthew's Virgil. My quest was at an end. I stood there staring at it for so long that I burnt myself with the torch. Then I turned and ran from the cave into the warm sunlight and beyond.
>
> In the centre of the book I found an envelope with my name on the outside. With trembling fingers I tore it open. There was a single sheet within, covered with the hermit's neat and small writing. There were general directions for gathering and preparing the herbs, for pulverising them and mixing them together, and then I saw in close writing a list of Roman names and numerals. The words danced before my eyes. I was almost overcome with excitement. Witch Hazel (Hamamelif Virginica XIII and v); Atropa Belladonna xv; Saxifraga (Herba)

xc and xii; Thymuf vii; Willow Herb (Epilobium) xx; Digitalis v . . .

It took Wilson until that October before he identified and found all the herbs required and made the concoction. There were strict instructions concerning its consumption. For the first six months, half a gill only was to be drunk every third day; thereafter only a gill was required every six months. To drink too much too soon would be to risk dire consequences. Wilson's diary entry for 12 February 1814 records his mistake in drinking his half-gill a day too early. Initially there was no problem but later that day he fell to the ground as if dead while on a training run on a path near Stayling. He was in a state of morbid paralysis due to the herbs, but nevertheless two local doctors independently certified death and his body was laid out for burial the next morning, at the Dick Turpin pub, where he could clearly hear the voice of old Bill Hardy, the landlord, issuing instructions.

There was another voice to ponder on as well. 'Good riddance to bad rubbish,' snarled the ever-cheerful Jasper Falby in the background as the crowd gathered. 'By dying he's saved us the trouble of shutting him up in the asylum.' It was wishful thinking, despite Wilson being taken to the village prison after waking from his paralysis. He soon used his incredible strength to bend two of the prison cell's window bars and was off into the wild. It was the beginning of a hectic, incident-packed time for young Wilson.

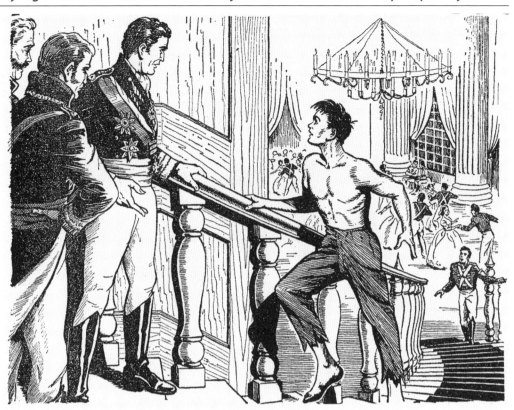

A DECISIVE MOMENT
Only now are details emerging of a stupendous 20-mile cross country run by the young Wilson to warn the Duke of Wellington that Napoleon was gathering his troops at Quatre Bras ahead of the Battle of Waterloo.

WILSON AT LARGE

On 11 April 1814 Wilson won the Stayling Easter Mile – from Gobbett Ash to Cold Brook Bridge, He had to join from the crowd a hundred yards behind the leaders on account of there being a warrant on his head after Jasper Falby declared him to be a vagrant. According to the incredulous local schoolteacher Roger Whacker, the only commoner in the village with a reliable timepiece, Wilson won in four minutes two seconds, forty-three seconds quicker than the existing record and a time so incredible that many onlookers dismissed it as being pure fantasy.

He then fled to Europe for the first time, on a packet ship from Folkestone to Boulogne. The weather was extremely rough and the ship was unable to dock safely, so Wilson, along with his rucksack, leapt an astonishing 26 feet or more from the ship to the Wharf.

Next came Brussels and a mind-blowing do- or- die cross-country run from Quatre Bras back to the Duke of Wellington's ball in Brussels to warn him that Napoleon was gathering his troops. The prior warning this afforded Wellington is retrospectively considered to have been decisive in both the Battle of Quatre Bras and at Waterloo shortly afterwards. The eminent historian Edward Cotton makes no mention of the incident in his otherwise definitive account of the Battle of Waterloo, *A Voice From Waterloo* (published 1854). But Wilson himself recalled that Wellington's reaction to his dispatch was so tumultuous and swift that there was no time even to leave his name and details with Wellington's chief of staff. In addition Wilson, aged only twenty, was already displaying a dislike for publicity and attention. It is a trait that has remained constant throughout his life.

THEY BELIEVED HE MUST BE SUPERNATURAL, NOT OF THIS WORLD
When two hunters high on the slopes of the Jungfrau witnessed Wilson outrun one of the Chamois they had been hunting, they gathered a posse and arrested him.

So, without a backward glance, he travelled to Switzerland and a harsh mountain habitat in which he felt completely at home. Soon after he arrived, however, he was arrested on suspicion of being a werewolf! Two disbelieving chamois hunters had witnessed him outrun one of their prey high on the Jungfrau. So astonished were they by the spectacle, they believed that he must be supernatural, not of this world. The consequences of such accusations could be dire . . .

Wilson was marched by a dozen musketeers into the village of Lauterbrunnen and taken to a deep, icy pool where a thunderous waterfall flowed from the mountain stream. Over the centuries the villagers had developed a test to determine whether the accused was man or beast. He would be thrown into the pool – which was known as the Demon's Pool. If he was human, he would still be alive after an hour; werewolves could not swim. The waters were not hospitable, though, and only one man had ever survived the test.

In he plunged. Wilson was in his element and frolicked happily in the icy pool for not just one but five hours, regularly refusing the offer of a rope, before admitting that he was a little chilly. Despite his aversion to publicity, Wilson was, on occasions, a showman *par excellence*. The classic extrovert–introvert who only truly comes alive when performing? Perhaps. There is definitely a theatrical side to his nature. A feast was held in his honour but Wilson, ever the spartan, did not want to compromise his fitness by over-indulging; he ate and drank sparingly before escaping back to the mountains and his beloved Jungfrau at 4 a.m., while the rest of the village slept.

His 'Grand Tour' continued to Venice. He arrived there in October 1816 and settled for five years in the city of lovers though, as ever, there is no mention of a romantic interest for Wilson. With an abundance of testosterone coursing through his veins you would suspect this might have been an issue but, as with many superheroes, women don't appear to feature highly in his exploits. For a long time sex was deemed to hinder athletic performance – boxers have always abstained before big fights and athletes were advised to practise monastic self-restraint before a race. This theory was later blown sky-high when both Bob Beamon and Lasse Viren admitted to bouts of love-making before world record performances.

Anyway how could any woman become involved with a man who, every night, silently lapped the Grand Canal and, having swum 12 miles before dawn, continued his studies into medicine and wider culture? In the absence of running opportunities, Wilson concentrated on refining his jumping techniques. He attained notoriety, and the lasting gratitude of the Prince of Piedmont after leaping across the 26 foot Ponzine Canal off three or four paces to rescue the Venetian aristocrat from would-be assassins. Many have tried the leap since and come to a wet end.

Having been away for seven years, he arrived back in England just days after his twenty-sixth birthday, on 3 November 1821. Landing in Dover, he then jog-trotted the 200 miles to Ambleside, often running in the lee of travelling stagecoaches to make things a little easier (even Wilson allowed himself the occasional off day). The journey did have its moments of drama, though – at one point along the way he successfully chased three highwaymen, running down their horses after they had stolen goods from Sir Mumford Poulton, whose coach they had hijacked.

When he reached Stayling, he immediately ran into his arch-enemy, the tyrannical Jasper Falby who, to make matters worse, was now the village squire. All power corrupts and absolute power corrupts absolutely, and Squire Falby was certainly no exception to the rule. The village was desolate and in ruins. Poverty was universal, and the rent he now charged was astronomical.

Enraged, Wilson immediately hatched a plan to engineer Squire Falby's downfall. He wagered a thousand pounds of his personal wealth that he could better the legendary javelin throw of Jasper's ancestor 'Black' Falby. Once the strongest man in Yorkshire, in 1515 he threw a bronze Roman javelin 260 feet from the terrace of Falby Manor. The javelin had become a Falby family heirloom, and a commemoration stone in Long Meadow marked the exact spot it had landed. In the unlikely event of Wilson being successful, Jasper agreed to lower the rents to the levels they were under his more benevolent father.

Wilson allowed himself nine days to prepare for this challenge, taking to the moor for inspiration, and experimenting around the clock to perfect his technique using a collection of home-made javelins. Remember there could be no run-up for the throw; he had to perfect his stance and find ways of building momentum from a stationary position.

On the day itself he allowed himself six dummy swings. The gathered crowd wondered if he was ever going to release the implement. Then, suddenly, he swayed back six inches further than before, tensed every muscle – smooth relaxed tendons became iron girders – and with a primeval roar unleashed a mighty throw. The howl alarmed some onlookers, but was a technique that he knew to be prevalent in Nordic countries; the conscious and deliberate expulsion of air was said to stimulate the muscles and the mind. The javelin launched into the sky like a heat-seeking missile and finally landed a staggering 24 feet beyond the stone. His popularity had never been higher among the village folk but Wilson hadn't finished yet.

While Wilson had been overseas, Jasper had illegally annexed the village's common land, some 1280 acres which was used for grazing and herding livestock. Flushed by his javelin success, Wilson now embarked on a high-risk double

WITH ONE MIGHTY LEAP
While studying and training in Venice, Wilson leapt the width of the famous Ponzine Canal – some 26 feet – to rescue the Prince of Piedmont, who was being attacked by would-be assassins. Nobody has repeated the feat.

SQUIRE FALBY'S DOWNFALL
Wilson tests the weight and balance of the bronze Roman javelin he threw 260 feet, without a run-up, to win a wager against the wicked Squire Falby, who had been terrorizing his villagers.

or quits strategy. He upped his wager to two thousand pounds and the challenge was to run around the perimeter of the common land – in excess of six miles over extremely rough

HE REACHED THE FINISH LINE WITH JUST TWO SECONDS REMAINING
The second part of the wager with Squire Falby saw Wilson run around the perimeter of the tyrant's estate in less than 30 minutes to claim the land for the village. Falby reneged on the bet, with dire consequences.

terrain – in less than thirty minutes. Any ground covered in addition to the common ground perimeter would also be claimed by the people of Stayling as common land.

It was a monumental effort, clearly beyond mere mortal men. But Wilson, the supreme athlete, added a novel twist. With ten minutes left to go, the spectators just beginning to dare to believe that he could succeed, he suddenly veered out on an unexpected mile and half loop which was clearly intended to include Squire Falby's manor! The audacity of the man! Madness, surely? Somehow, drawing on reserves of strength hitherto unsuspected even by Wilson himself, he reached the finish line with just two seconds remaining on the stopwatch. Incredible. Falby was enraged, and though he honoured the first part of the bargain by handing back the common land he refused point blank to give up the manor. He also instigated a manhunt for Wilson, at one time snaring him in a lethal man trap on the moor – but of course Wilson had the pure brute strength to disentangle himself.

Wilson took a decidedly poor view of such dastardly conduct and some weeks later, having made the decision to leave Ambleside for the even more remote hills of Cleveland, he decided to bid a memorable farewell to Falby. Late one dark night he worked like a gang of twenty navvies high above the manor damming up the river with massive stone boulders and diverting it into the valley below. By two o'clock the next morning the task was complete and by breakfast time the manor – the sole habitation in that beautiful valley – was under three feet of water. Revenge is a dish best served cold.

Wilson's Cleveland Years are little chronicled, though he was happy with the anonymity and solitude that the hills provided, and his remarkable powers continued to develop. It seems that there is only so much human contact he could tolerate and intermittently he needed to disappear, recharge his batteries and,

WILSON RECOVERED IN STYLE
Though not a man of violence, Wilson always enjoyed boxing as one of the ultimate tests of fitness and skill. In 1833, while in London, he overcame an early cheap shot from Jem Sprigg to rout the champion prizefighter.

perhaps, nurture his spiritual side as well. It was a tactical retreat in his campaign to live forever and to challenge the limits of human achievement.

It was a chance meeting with two old-style sportsmen, Squire Pickering and Lord Newton, that re-ignited his competitive instincts. Firstly he beat them in a race from Pickering to Thirsk – him on foot while they rode a team of horses – and while celebrating his win later that night he amazed them by hurling a 16-pound shot fully 70 feet across the dining room and through the wall into Squire Pickering's study. An indoor world record, for sure.

They persuaded him to travel south to London where they wanted to showcase his talents – and place considerable wagers on the side. Wilson, being Wilson, appears to have made the 200 mile journey on foot, taking twenty-six hours and thirty minutes.

Once there, Wilson trained assiduously for nine months, and in 1833 Pickering decided that it was time to introduce Wilson to London's sporting society. His first fight was against Jem Sprigg, the champion prizefighter. Despite being knocked nearly senseless with one early blow, Wilson recovered to win in fine style.

While in London, deprived of his beloved moorland on which to run, he had been concentrating on his upper body strength, which paid off a couple of months later in a double-header against the legendary Irish strongman O'Shea, then considered to be the finest thrower of the weight (shot) and hammer in all of Europe.

First came the hammer and, though O'Shea was a worthy opponent, he was outclassed by Wilson who hurled it a record 250 feet on his third and final attempt. He was angered, however, by an orchestrated outburst of coughing and shouting by O'Shea supporters as he made his vital turns, and angrily sought Pickering and Newton to register his displeasure. 'There's going to be trouble,' warned Wilson. 'That cheer was organised to put me off my throw. Someone put them up to it. There's big money on O'Shea. Betting ruins sport, I tell you.'

His two backers made soothing noises, but they were scarcely blameless themselves, having ventured massive amounts of money on their man. Wilson, whose attitude seems slightly hypocritical, as he wasn't averse to a wager, was not mollified. For a while he considered withdrawing from the contest altogether, before even attempting the shot. In the end however, red with rage, he marched to the circle and hurled the shot 81 feet 3 inches, a Beamonesque performance which to this day has never been bettered.

Wilson was disgusted with the betting and result-fixing that he was witnessing in the sporting world, and once again he headed for the hills, travelling this time to the Highlands of Scotland – more specifically, to the rugged and beautiful Ben Mor region of Sutherland. There he recovered his equanimity and lived in blissful isolation for nearly twenty years, training and running every day and refining his diet. There was one dimly-remembered incident when an

DRAMATIC RESCUE ON BEN MOR
Wilson was a brilliant and natural climber with many unrecorded first ascents. He also used his mountaineering skills to save an Oxford graduate who was caught out by bad weather in the remote Scottish hills.

Oxbridge climbing type, unaccustomed to the severity of the Scottish hills, became stranded at the top of a mountain after an epic climb and Wilson was forced to ascend in a blizzard and then return down the rock face with the climber clinging to his back. The rest of the time there passed in silence until in, 1852, at the age of fifty-six but with the honed physique of a twenty-five-year-old, he again grew restless for human company and turned up unannounced at the Highland Games, effortlessly beating all comers, before slipping characteristically away when the feasting and fun began that night. Pining for Ambleside after so many years away, he began jog-trotting south.

THE TRUTH ABOUT WILSON

'LOOK OUT,' WILSON SHOUTED, 'THERE'S A MONSTER COMING!'

So reclusive had Wilson become that when he decided to travel to London, running along a strange railed track he had come upon, he was alarmed to be chased by an iron monster belching steam. Trains could be very frightening for the uninitiated!

Wilson's journey south was nothing if not eventful. As he set out, under cover of darkness, he stumbled across strange parallel steel rods with planks of wood placed between them at regular intervals – and they were heading in the very direction he sought. It was as if some benevolent force had laid out a personal running track for him! He set off happily into the night, averaging between nine and ten miles an hour, but became aware of a strange hissing and belching noise behind him. As he peered back into the darkness, he could just about make out the orange glow of fire emanating from a strange, dark beast – a puffing iron monster or a demon! He set off down the track again, this time at a sprint, the beast hot on his trail. Wilson offers no explanation as to why he simply didn't quit the track and climb up the embankment to escape his pursuer. Wilson was not a vain man but he clearly possessed a massive sporting ego, so it is likely that on this occasion, though a little scared, his competitive instincts again took over. Whatever it was that dogged his every step he was going to race it. Perhaps it's worth stating the blindingly obvious to say so, but as well as being an exceptional gifted, supremely athletic, hardy and driven man, Wilson is also clearly quite mad in that quin-tessentially eccentric British manner. We should always expect unusual behaviour from him, and in that he rarely disappoints.

Finally Wilson and his pursuer reached what appeared to be a small habitation alongside the track. He ran through it at pace and was startled to see a man standing on a platform

SPORTING SUCCESS AT THE INTERNATIONAL INVITATION MEETING, CRYSTAL PALACE

Wilson announced his return from his wilderness years in the Scottish Highlands with a world record leg of 1 minute 46 seconds for the 880 yards in the medley relay. He later won the shot putt left-handed after his right hand had been broken by a German competitor.

in uniform. It had to be four o'clock in the morning. 'Look out,' Wilson shouted. 'There's a monster coming!'

When he looked back, however, the monster had stopped, and all appeared peaceful and benign. Then, to his bemusement, people started climbing in and out of the belly of the beast, laughing and joking as they went. This was all very strange. He spoke the man in uniform who revealed the truth. This was a locomotive steam train, a recent invention designed to transport citizens at high speed around the country. Wilson felt like a prize fool, but if nothing else it confirmed his decision to quit Scotland. He had been out of touch for too long. It was time to return to the real world.

Back at Ambleside, once again almost the first person he bumped into was Squire Jasper Falby, now a sorry figure confined to a wheelchair after years suffering from consumption and gout. Wilson couldn't resist a dig: 'High living doesn't seem to have agreed with you Jasper You ought to have lived the simple life like me and you'd have kept young.'

You will excuse me if I don't dwell on his feats of athleticism during this era, exceptional as they were, but there is much more ground to cover. It would be remiss, however, not to mention an extraordinary 10-mile swim ashore in rough conditions to organise help for a stricken paddle steamer travelling between Hull and London. The attendant publicity was again a nuisance for Wilson, and there is evidence that he went to ground for a year or more in Norwich before finally heading back to London again in 1854.

Once there, he agreed to compete for Parrington Harriers, under the assumed name of William Williams, at the International Invitational Meeting at Norwood Hill, part of the sparkling new Crystal Palace complex that had been built after the Great Exhibition of 1851. His 880-yard leg in the medley relay was timed by hand at one minute forty-six seconds – and was deemed to be an unofficial world record. This caused much comment, but Wilson's afternoon was not yet over. He had only intended to compete in the relay, until he overheard a conversation between a group of burly German and Scandinavian types.

'At running the British are always best,' said the biggest and ugliest of the continental field event competitors. 'We have no chance against them at running. They have had so much practice running away from their enemies.'

Wilson was not amused. 'There was a burst of laughter at that and I turned on my heel and made straight for the secretary's office to enter the field events as well,' the great man recalled in his diaries. Britain's reputation clearly had to be defended and who better to take up the challenge? There followed a remarkable explosion of athletic excellence that hinted at his decathlon world record nearly a century later.

Within the space of a couple of hours he long-jumped 26 feet and soared to an amazing 6 feet 11 inches in the high jump even before the throwing events were staged. The big ugly German referred to earlier successfully crushed Wilson's right hand and broke two fingers when he offered his 'sincere' congratulations, but Wilson was not to be deterred. He responded by throwing the shot a staggering 58 feet 6 inches, left-handed, to win that event and though struggling with his injury and techniques in the first two rounds of the hammer, he rallied magnificently to post a new world record of 195 feet.

As ever though there was a price to pay. 'William Williams' was lauded and feted, though very soon people started to make the connection between him and Wilson. Life became intolerable under the public gaze and, now fifty-nine years old, he once again ran for the hills, this time to remote Axmoor in the West Country where he lives to this day. His privacy is protected by the local community who recognise his need for space and solitude, interrupted by bursts of frantic activity when the urge to perform and excel takes over.

Though Axmoor became his permanent base, Wilson wandered extensively through Spain and Portugal during the next two decades, immersing himself in their cultures. There then follows a strange, and very long interlude, in which Wilson seems preoccupied with living a life of solitude and harbouring his extraordinary physical talents. He has not written of this period, or if he has we have yet to discover the material. Remember, now aged seventy and living in a time when sixty was considered ancient, he would ordinarily have been expecting to be at the end of his days. These will have been tense times as he waited to see if the elixir really did work. The run-up to his one hundredth birthday was to be completely unknown territory.

Sightings became extremely rare. There was one report of a British soldier, mistakenly imprisoned and sentenced to death in Bordeaux during the Franco-Prussian War, who escaped the firing squad by jumping a 6 foot 10 inch brick wall off a three pace run-up . This was almost certainly Wilson – not bad, in fairness, for a man of seventy-five – but there the trail goes cold. It seems probable that he occupied much of his time coaching others and nurturing outstanding British talent.

THE HALCYON YEARS

Wilson seems to have truly blossomed in the years just either side of the Second World War, when he fully harnessed all of his amazing abilities. With track and field now properly organised and established as a sport, gambling having been banned, and Britain's national honour to be upheld, it truly was his time to shine.

And at last he had a Boswell to his Johnson. W.S.K. Webb, whose appearance on the scene was timely and valuable both as a witness who would record Wilson's achievements during those years for posterity, and as a historian of this remarkable man's life and times. To offer you a flavour of the period, I quote from the early passages of *The Truth About Wilson*, Webb's chronicle of the time:

> No more sensational figure ever appeared in sporting history. His name was on the lips of even those who ordinarily had not the least interest in athletics. The photographs of this amazing man were published all over the world. Films in which he appeared flashed on the screens of cinemas from Melbourne to Valparaiso.
>
> Wilson was news. Everything that Wilson did, every fact that could be gleaned about Wilson was red-hot news. The names of but few athletes appear anywhere except in the sporting pages of newspapers. But Wilson

A NEW WORLD RECORD
Wilson perfected the 'Fosbury Flop' many decades before the American athlete Dick Fosbury introduced the technique at the 1968 Olympics. Note, however, that Wilson has only a sandpit to land in. Contemporary reports suggest he actually completed a backward somersault to prevent injury.

was front-page stuff. He smashed athletics records like cheap crockery and set standards that will never be equalled, let alone surpassed.

Wilson's 'golden era' started in 1938 at the British Championships at Stamford Bridge where a record crowd of some 80,000 had gathered for what had been billed as a one-day Olympics – how UK athletics would kill for such a gate these days! The mile, as ever, was the main attraction, with the American Ron Gleebe expected to break his own world record of four minutes five seconds. Wilson was not entered and only joined the race – as the thirteenth man – by vaulting over the barriers and onto the start line a fraction after the starting gun was fired. He was wearing the all-in-one black running garment that was soon to be renowned worldwide.

The race that followed defied belief. Wilson appeared to be sprinting rather than pacing himself, recording 57 seconds for the first 440 yards, and he continued in a similar vein. As he entered the final lap, everybody assumed he would 'hit the wall' and collapse. But not a bit of it. He kept going magnificently and hit the tape at three minutes forty-eight seconds, a full seventeen seconds inside the world record. The world had never seen anything like it, and his time would remain unmatched in Britain until the arrival of Seb Coe, Steve Ovett and Steve Cram. He collapsed into the familiar post-race coma of exhaustion before making a full recovery

and disappearing from the heaving stadium. Wilson was back!

Three weeks later he made a late appearance at the international meeting at the Bellevue Stadium where Great Britain were taking on the USA, Italy, Germany, Finland and France. He missed the 1500 metres but was a late entry in the high jump, and astounded everyone watching by creating a new world record of 7 foot 1 inch with an old-style western roll, without even grazing the bar. Afterwards he teased the assembled gentlemen of the press a little by saying he was only emulating the Dalesman Roderick Ferguson, who had jumped a wall measured at 7 foot 1 inch at Stayling on 17 March 1832.

At the Athens Games soon afterwards, he completed a unique classical double by winning the marathon in two hours twenty minutes despite starting late and, after travelling to the island of Lathos to study a statue of the Greek javelin-thrower Ermes, he also took the javelin with a throw of 262 feet. The distance was down a little on his effort of 1821 but modern javelins were heavier, and the centre of gravity had been altered to reduce distances so that the competition could take place within a stadium

New York was next and Wilson clocked forty-four seconds dead-on for the 440 yards, despite running with three broken ribs. He followed this a fortnight later with a world record time of nine seconds in the 100 yards.

The following year in Germany, with war looming, it was a matter of national pride that Britain perform well at the

WILSON THE FLYING ACE

Wilson, as you would expect, was one of the 'Few'. He was awarded a DFC and bar for his exploits as a fighter pilot in World War Two, shooting down 24 enemy aircraft. He is also rumoured to have turned down a VC because of the attendant publicity.

prestigious Golden Eagle relay event attended by Dr Goebbels, Germany's Minister for Propaganda and an unlikely athletics fan. Suspecting that the Germans were illegally using drugs to enhance their performances, Wilson was on his mettle and recorded two of the greatest runs in history, although as hand-timed relay legs they were not universally considered to be world records. Nobody in Britain needed to be convinced, however – Frank Ducker was regarded as the most impartial and objective timekeeper in the sport. He had Wilson down for a 440-yard relay leg of forty-two seconds (Michael Johnson territory),and an even more astounding one minute forty seconds for the 880 yards.

That was the last hurrah before Wilson and his party escaped from Germany into France on the very day war was declared, returning to London to sign up, as was the duty of every able-bodied man. As they travelled back Ducker caught a tantalising glimpse of a couple of phrases jotted down by Wilson in his diary, which he committed to memory. It is just as well, because Wilson did not allow them to be published as part of his diary extracts after the war:

Fitness must be of the body and the brain. The brain must always be the director. The body cannot be hard if the mind plays with thoughts of warmth and comfort.

Man can be his own master. There is nothing he cannot do if he has the determination to do it.

My system neutralises the poisons that age and kill, replaces the tissues that are worn, revives the blood stream and perpetuates youth.

A much overlooked part of Wilson's life was his heroic service with the RAF in the Second World War, having enlisted immediately on his return from competing during the late summer of 1939. Now at the age of 144 he trained to fly Spitfires and Hurricanes, and it will come as no surprise to those who appreciate his tremendous dexterity and hand-eye coordination that he proved an outstanding fighter pilot, and very quickly earned the Distinguished Flying Cross and bar for 'an act or acts of valour, courage or devotion to duty whilst flying in active operations against the enemy. Indeed RAF veterans insist that he should have been awarded a Victoria Cross after an incident in which, while under heavy enemy fire, he climbed onto the wing of a Lancaster bomber to extinguish an engine fire and save his eleven crew members. However, Wilson made it quite clear he would walk away from all flying duties if his name were to be put forward.

His skills were put to the ultimate test in September 1940 during the Battle of Britain when he recorded the majority of his total of 24 confirmed kills, often flying three or four sorties a day. Wilson's total sees him just creep into the top ten of British Second World War aces, a list headed by Jonny Johnson, on 36, with the Anglo-Irishman Brendan Finucane coming next on 32. Wilson is just one ahead of Douglas Bader, who will always be remembered as the fighter pilot with artificial legs, who had a total of 23. Like Wilson he was destined to end up as a prisoner of war.

During this time of heightened tensions, it wasn't only Wilson's courage and skills as a pilot that saw him shine but his incredible stamina and physical reserves. He was not tempted by the excesses to be found in the mess tent. While colleagues in his squadron partied at the Red Bull pub and chased local girls he chose to spend his spare time updating his diary and reading texts on the ancient Greek Olympics.

Wilson's luck ran out one day flying over the North Sea. He came under attack by no fewer than five Messerschmitt 109s as he went to assist a colleague who was trying to get back home with only one functioning engine. He stood no chance and, as his plane caught fire, he cut himself free, managing to bale out just in time.

The frenzied attack had taken him off the beaten track and when he splashed down he was 24 miles north-west of the Dutch coast; a long swim even for Wilson, although, naturally, he was in peak condition. Wilson discarded his clinging uniform and struck out, eventually reaching a deserted beach where he stumbled across the body of a dead British airman named Corporal Greene. Wilson had no particular need for Greene's clothing in terms of warmth, but he quickly realised that, if he was captured while wearing a uniform, he would be able to claim rights under the Geneva Convention – while if he were discovered in a state of semi-nakedness he would probably be shot as a spy.

Despite his superhuman efforts to evade capture he was eventually found by a crack SS outfit and sent to a POW camp. While making that lonely journey it occurred to him that this was the perfect opportunity to give the press the slip once and for all – he could steal Corporal Greene's identity, discard the Wilson persona, and finally be free. One has to assume that even Wilson was operating under extreme stress at this period of his life but nonetheless it seems a strange and quixotic decision – had he even thought of Greene's family's reaction when he arrived back in Britain and started competing under that name? It is one area of the Wilson story that just doesn't feel right and it warrants further investigation. We know from conversations with POW colleagues that he kept a diary at this period, but that valuable historical document has not yet been found.

During his imprisonment he befriended Ray Vale, a brilliant young athlete and airman who had almost lost a leg during his own wartime 'prang'. Wilson patiently nursed him back to full fitness, organising his physical rehabilitation and collecting those herbs that grew naturally and surprisingly abundantly within the camp.

Vale returned to competitive athletics on his repatriation with notable success on the county circuit and Wilson continued to blaze a trail, first as Corporal Greene and then as himself! Displaying a rather perverse sense of humour in his new persona he set about astounding the athletics commun-ity with a series of outstanding performances that can only be described as, well, Wilsonian. By now one or two more discerning critics were beginning to make the connection when his hand was forced anyway.

An unscrupulous journalist, one Edelston Linter, was making a small fortune with his best-selling book *How to be a Wilson*, in which he claimed intimate knowledge of the training methods and lifestyle of the dead war hero and former athlete. Wilson was enraged and, in a famous episode we reproduce in this book, set about proving that the real

Wilson was alive. Suffice to say at this juncture that by the summer of 1946 the sporting community was rejoicing with the news that Wilson was indeed alive and very well indeed. Of course there were many who suddenly claimed never to have believed the reports of his death in the first place. It was inconceivable, surely, that the 'Amazing Wilson' would ever come off second best against the 'Hun'.

THE BLACK OLYMPICS

Many have commented on Wilson's mysterious absence from the 1948 London Olympics when, at the height of his powers, he seemed ideally placed to restore the morale and optimism of the nation after the Second World War with a clutch of gold medals and world records. Now, nearly sixty years later, we can at last reveal the extraordinary truth behind his non-attendance. He was in central Africa at the time, engaged in the immeasurably more important task of fighting to preserve the British Empire. Political sensitivity still means that only the outline of this breathtaking story can be recounted at this juncture.

Chaka, the chief of the Zulus, was determined to oust all the colonizing 'whites' from Africa. He decided it would be a good ploy to rouse and inspire the indigenous population with an event that would pit Britain's top athletes against his best warriors, thus demonstrating the athletic superiority of his tribesmen. To that end, he had ordered the kidnap of our very finest sportsmen, Wilson included.

The kidnap attempt on Wilson failed – unsurprisingly he comfortably outran the three warriors sent to Britain to abduct him – but after a clandestine meeting with some of Whitehall's 'top brass', it was decided that he should *allow* himself to be abducted, along with the ever reliable AAA official Frank Ducker, and transported to Africa apparently at Chaka's behest. Once there, the stakes were high: the lives of the kidnapped British athletes rested entirely on Wilson's success – or failure – in each event. For every Wilson win, an athlete would be spared. There followed, over a period of months, a series of heroic performances as Wilson defeated all of Chaka's champions one by one in their individual events.

In a double or quits move Chaka then sent for the Congolese decathlete Masa, to challenge Wilson to a head-to-head in front of 250,000 tribesmen who had been promised a celebratory feast before waging war. Wilson upped the ante further by suggesting the event include a tug of war between the eight kidnapped British athletes, himself included, and eight Zulu warriors.

Wilson trained all night every night to hone his fitness and come the big day he was in peak condition. The most memorable event was the long jump – Masa began the competition by challenging him to jump over thirty warriors

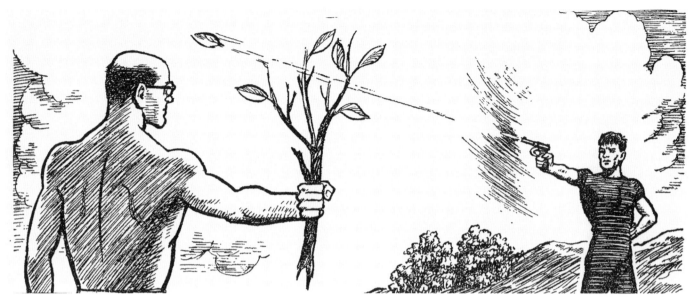

A COMPLETE NOVICE, HE EMBARKED ON A CRASH COURSE IN SHOOTING

As he trained for the 1952 Olympics, Wilson was an obvious candidate for the Modern Pentathlon, but first he had to learn how to shoot. A complete novice, he embarked on a crash course. Having a colleague hold the target apparently helped him concentrate!

lying prone on the ground. Both men accomplished that easily, prompting Wilson to suggest that they attempt forty – and this time the warriors should hold their razor-sharp spears pointed at 90 degrees into the air. While Masa refused to attempt the jump, Wilson sailed clear. Wilson had routed the Congolese athlete, and soon the crowd were jeering both Masa and Chaka.

To rub salt into the wound Wilson's team of spindly middle distance and marathon runners then used superior technique to defeat the Zulu musclemen in the tug of war, and to top it all off the rotund Ducker, (now nearer the age of seventy than sixty, but trained by Wilson in the technicalities of the event), challenged Chaka to a javelin competition – and won by a yard! Chaka was last seen sneaking out of the arena in disgrace. On his return, Wilson was offered an OBE by a grateful government, but declined the honour and was never heard to speak of his African experiences for the rest of his career.

<hr />

MODERN PENTATHLON GOLD

<hr />

After missing out on the 1948 Olympics in London while serving Britain and the Empire so commendably in Africa, Wilson was determined to compete in Helsinki four years later. He could have commanded a place in the British athletics team in any event he chose. Athletics, however, is invariably high-profile and, as we have seen, Wilson struggled with life in the public eye throughout his long career. Instead, he chose the Modern Pentathlon, a classic

all-rounder's event but one that rarely receives many column inches. He was also keen to indulge his lifelong love of horses, and with these twin objectives in mind secured a job as a groom at Loamhead, where the British Olympic equestrian team was based.

As for the modern pentathlon, running and swimming would be a walk in the park as far as Wilson was concerned, and he was also a natural horseman, though he had ridden little in the previous hundred years. He was, however, a complete novice at shooting and fencing. To stand any chance of winning, he had to embark on a crash course in both, whilst keeping up with his day job of caring for Britain's finest three-day event and showjumping horses. In separate conversations with Captain Webb and Frank Ducker, Wilson was insistent that his quiet months spent at Major Howe's establishment during were the happiest of his life.

His adventures en route to the gold medal are worthy of a book in their own right, and it is possible we will consider such a publication, but for now we will concentrate on the five days of competition in Helsinki. Fortunes on the first day were mixed. When his horse was spooked by a high-pitched screech from the crowd, Wilson was thrown, badly wrenching a shoulder, but recovered brilliantly to finish in eighth place. Later a British camp follower, one Stanley Verricker, who wore a monocle, was exposed as the villain and immediately deported for sabotaging Wilson's ride.

Wilson spent the subsequent night bathing in an icy pond to lessen the damage and free his shoulder from the worst of the injury, but not before having to make a flying visit to the Helsinki Harbour Police, who had arrested an immensely promising young British runner named Alf Tupper, who had worked his passage to Finland as a cook's assistant on a

SOMEHOW WILSON HAD TO WIN

In a tactical masterstroke Wilson made up for his lack of technical ability as a fencer by using his legendary fitness to make the fights last as long as possible and tire out his two main opponents.

for the overall title were Subadar, the dashing Indian army officer, and the American Baylor. They were both international fencers in their own right as well as being talented swimmers and runners, and leading the field in showjumping. Somehow Wilson, a newcomer to the sport, had to beat them or surrender his medal chances.

He achieved this with a brilliant and cunning double whammy, which is still spoken about in awed tones by pentathletes today. Wilson's advantage was his supreme athleticism. Against Subadar and Baylor he initially defended and parried brilliantly to avoid them landing the match-winning strike but gradually the pressure eased, as they grew

merchant ship. Wilson happily vouched for Tupper, wished him well, and then returned to his rehabilitation regime.

The next day was, tactically and physically, possibly Wilson's finest hour. All thirty-two competitors had to fence against each other, each contestant taking between three or four minutes; a truly gruelling day's sport. The two favourites

breathless and fatigued. Despite his injured shoulder Wilson was utterly unmoved and there came a point where he could have taken the initiative. Instead he chose to prolong their agony – ten, fifteen, twenty, twenty-five minutes, the clock ticked by and his opponents screamed in pain and discomfort.

WILSON— THE 1952 EXPLOITS OF THE AGELESS SUPER ATHLETE.

THE YEAR OF THE SHATTERED STUMPS

LIKE A THUNDERBOLT THE BALL WILSON BOWLED ROSE OVER THE STUMPS AND FIELDERS

When in full flow Wilson could bowl at 120mph and the summer of 1953 in England is noted for a succession of shattered sightscreens around the country, the result of some express deliveries hitting them first bounce.

He finally finished them off on the half hour. Neither Subadar nor Baylor could muster any energy in their subsequent bouts and they finished way down the field in an event they should have been dominating. Only the fabulous French fencer André Mourrier could beat Wilson that day. Thereafter life was much simpler – he won the swimming, covering 300 metres in three minutes with his sixteen leg beats to one stroke method; performed creditably in the shooting; and routed all comers in the cross-country run though he started a minute behind after tarrying to ensure the temperamental Sir Lancelot was happy and relaxed for his gold medal round with Major Howe in the showjumping.

⬦⬦⬦⬦⬦⬦⬦⬦⬦⬦⬦⬦⬦⬦⬦⬦⬦⬦⬦⬦⬦⬦

WILSON WINS THE ASHES FOR ENGLAND

⬦⬦⬦⬦⬦⬦⬦⬦⬦⬦⬦⬦⬦⬦⬦⬦⬦⬦⬦⬦⬦⬦

Wilson's swansong – for the time being at least, as it seems inconceivable that even at the age of 217, he will be able to resist the lure of the 2012 London Olympics – came in the tumultuous summer of 1953 when he secured a famous Ashes win against Australia in the final test at the Oval. It came just a year after his extraordinary gold medal in the Olympic Modern Pentathlon Championship and confirmed,

if any confirmation were needed, his legendary all-round status.

What a strange summer! It began when Captain Webb's successor, Duggy Rannoch, the *Clarion*'s no-nonsense, hard-drinking Scottish sports editor (no clichés there then!) called his cricket correspondent, Reg Webster, into his office and showed him a clipping from the *Western Argus* in which Leasford bowled out their neighbouring village Mingsford for 40, all of the runs coming in extras. Something very strange had happened and Rannoch wanted to know what.

Indeed it had. Wilson had returned to cricket just when the game needed him most. Five years earlier, the unbeatable 1948 Australians under Sir Donald Bradman had humiliated England, and the need for sporting revenge was tangible throughout the country. As if by popular demand he concentrated all his great energies that summer to bowl consistently at 120 miles per hour – some 20 miles per hour quicker than modern-day speedsters such as Shoaib Akhtar and Jeff Thomson.

Webster hurried to Leasford and spent the rest of the summer trailing Wilson who, as ever, was uncomfortable with the spotlight into which he was thrust by his amazing feats. While visiting Leasford CC, Webster discovered that one of the sightscreens had been broken almost in two by the force of Wilson's thunderbolts as they screamed through the wicket-keeper's gloves and onward to the boundary.

HIS CRICKET STUMPS ARE FORGED IRON

Buying new sets of stumps was becoming an expensive business for all the teams Wilson played for so, ever considerate and generous, he asked his local shoesmith to forge six stumps out of iron to put an end to the devastation he was wreaking.

Wilson was soon in demand and was selected for Stoneshire against the unbeaten Australians. Unbelievably, he bowled them out twice on the first day, taking eighteen wickets as the tourists were dismissed first for 32 and then, after Stoneshire had scraped together 64, a paltry 23.

That evening he sped off to play in another game, for Leasford, in their annual grudge match against Mere End who, as chance would have it, had guest Australian batsman Kenny Leas – a brilliant but volatile individual – playing for them. Leas had failed to make the original touring party and was in England only to contribute columns for one of the Sydney newspapers. During the match, he smashed an out-rageous half-century, the only recorded occasion that a batsman got the measure of Wilson. Typically, Wilson responded by clean bowling the brave Aussie and then clubbing a hurricane fifty to win the match for Leasford.

A strange footnote to this match is that Webster was also pressed into service for the depleted Mere End team, and received an awful bruise and a broken blood vessel when taking a blow to the leg from Wilson. The following morning, amid concerns for his life, an ambulance was hurriedly called, but Wilson had already carried the ailing reporter onto the moor, where he covered the wound in mud and then dosed him with herbal sedatives and watched over him for twenty-four hours in his cave. Webster awoke feeling refreshed and renewed.

The summer continued. In a uniquely special invitation match, Wilson captained a team of namesakes – unrelated Wilsons who happened to share his name – to a win over county champions Highshire, taking eight wickets and hitting the required 36 runs on his own. Afterwards he destroyed the world record for throwing a cricket ball by hurtling it exactly 200 yards – a distance that has never been bettered – and for which he was awarded a prize ham.

A popular cry went up for his inclusion in the first test at Trent Bridge, although not everybody was convinced. 'Can

HE PREFERRED HIS ANCIENT BAT

Wilson had runs to make. These sleek bats of the 1950s were all very well but couldn't hold a candle to his trusted curved blade from the 1850s. The fielders and umpire were too astonished to raise any serious objection.

WILSON BOWLS IN BARE FEET

For somebody who had spent his life running barefoot on the moor, the cumbersome modern-day cricket boots proved a serious hindrance. Wilson solved the problem by simply taking them off and handing them to the startled umpire.

we afford to pick Wilson?' argued more than one 'expert' . Their argument was that English cricket could not financially sustain a succession of one-day tests . A little presumptuous, perhaps, but it seems to illustrate the impact that Wilson was having.

Following a number of incidents, which we hope to be at liberty to reveal in subsequent editions of this book, Wilson was duly selected to play for England. First, though, he insisted on honouring a commitment to appear for Stoneshire against Ribbleshire. During that match he celebrated his England selection in style, scoring 152, including a century off 28 deliveries, which subsequently won him the Waterford Crystal decanter for one of the fastest centuries in history. By way of an encore he then recorded a match analysis of 18 wickets for 14 runs as the game ended.

En route to Nottingham for the England match, he and Webster lodged overnight at the Coach and Horses in Rune Dale. At around three o'clock in the morning, the establishment caught fire and Wilson ran 8 miles in 30 minutes to fetch the Ashbury fire brigade, arguably his greatest ever long distance run. His heroic task complete, he shocked onlookers by appearing to drop dead, only to rise, like Lazarus, during his post-mortem. But Wilson was apparently a broken man. He was last seen wading pathetically out into the dangerous rip currents off Pendine sands in South Wales, the final defiant gesture of Britain's finest ever sportsman. A nation mourned, but in truth he had enjoyed a monumental innings – and he was 158 years old if he was a day.

Back at Trent Bridge, England's cricketers battled on

magnificently without him, the game played in near silence as the tragedy of Wilson's apparent death sunk in. They bravely drew the match, and then went on to win a rare victory against the Australians at Lord's. They then lost at Old Trafford, but drew again at Headingley. As late August approached, the Ashes were still at stake but the nation was beginning to despair of ever beating the Aussies.

O ye of little faith! Of course Wilson wasn't dead, he was simply working his way back to fitness and form away from the limelight, employed anonymously as a groundsman at Marlborough College where he had occasionally taught a century earlier. Not wishing to attract any undue attention, he trained by night, erecting a single stump with a candle tied to the top of it in the middle of the college square, and bowling at it until dawn. Not until he hit six in a row, as verified by the ever-loyal and evidently nocturnal Webster, did Wilson declare himself fit to play in the test the following day.

The rest is history. Wilson claimed all twenty wickets to bowl Australia out twice. England won the game with an hour to spare on the first day. The last word, then as now, must rest with the splendid Webster who signed off his report as follows.

With the crowd on to the field, Wilson ran. With hats going up in the air and ticket holders standing on their feet, yelling incoherently, he bounded up the gangway, through the doorway, and mysteriously disappeared. Wilson had gone. Everybody was searching for him. He must have planned his escape, for he had vanished. At the moment of supreme triumph, with every honour waiting for him – even a knighthood was mentioned in

WILSON IS BANNED AFTER FIVE BALLS
Before he had fully perfected his action and method of delivery as a fast bowler, Wilson could prove nothing short than lethal. On at least one occasion he was banned from bowling to prevent further injury to the opposition.

recognition for what he had achieved in athletics and cricket – he had disappeared into the quiet anonymity that he had always sought.

*Footnote: It has recently come to light that a photograph of a figure resembling Wilson, with his homespun black all-in-one running costume, was taken by a Mexican agency photographer showing him coaching Bob Beamon moments before his historic 29 foot 2.5 inch leap in 1968. When I contacted the veteran photographer earlier this year (he now lives in some style in Los Angeles) to ask him about the shot, he told me that the mysterious figure he had photographed had visited him in his run-down apartment in Mexico City and paid him $300,000 in cash for the print and negative of the picture.

This episode would appear to suggest that Wilson was operating as a freelance coach in the late 1960s. The adoption of the revolutionary 'Fosbury Flop' by Olympic high jump champion Dick Fosbury would add weight to this argument: the method, of course, had been pioneered by Wilson in the immediate postwar period. We can, however, dismiss stories that Harry Wilson – the coach behind the phenomenal success of Steve Ovett – was in any way related or connected to William Wilson.

BUT WHEN HE GOT IT RIGHT . . .
There was no more glorious sight in cricket, an action that was part Fred Trueman, part Jeff Thomson. Opposition batsmen could only shudder. Note the bandaged stumps, as the cricket authorities would not allow the metal stumps in Test matches.

Wilson and Tupper
— The day two Running Legends met

As hinted at earlier, the paths of two of British sport's legendary figures – William Wilson and Alf Tupper – did cross just once though, alas, it wasn't to run competitively against each other. It has been long rumoured that on that one occasion Wilson passed on the secret of the fabled elixir to Tupper, but it is, alas, untrue. What really happened? The truth can now, finally, be revealed for the first time.

William Wilson and Alf Tupper, Tough of the Track, met in 1952, firstly in the build-up to the Helsinki Olympics and then in Finland under the unusual circumstances described earlier. Wilson has a high regard for Tupper and though the British selectors considered Alf only an outside bet for an Olympic place, Wilson begged to differ and stated confidently that he would win the gold medal if given the opportunity.

The story of Tupper's try-out for the Great Britain Olympic team is incredible. En route to the 1500 metre Olympic trials at White City, he had been witness to a terrible rail accident just outside London, a crash which resulted in forty-seven fatalities and numerous casualties. He had worked tirelessly for thirty-six hours straight, cutting survivors free from the wreckage, before hitch-hiking directly on to participate in the trials, without any rest whatsoever. Tupper looked drawn and ill on arrival, but ran with typical courage to hang on and win the race before collapsing on the finishing line, apparently dead. The shocked crowd had no inkling of his heroic deeds the previous night, and indeed the two doctors at the scene could feel no pulse and pronounced him dead. Wilson, who had been watching incognito, rushed over and also took Tupper's pulse and was not so sure.

The following day Wilson and W.S.K. Webb drove to St Myram's Hospital, where the body had been taken, only to see a rather rejuvenated Tupper running away! Wilson was not surprised; 'His heart went to sleep. It didn't stop beating of course but the beat was so soft it wasn't perceptible. I have heard of eastern mystics doing something similar.'

They persuaded Tupper to return to hospital for further examination but the following morning he was gone for good. Eventually Wilson contacted Webb and told him to travel to Mardale in the New Forest the following morning. The ever-faithful Ducker also insisted on joining the party.

As Webb and Ducker surveyed the scene that shimmering early summer morning, they saw two figures speeding across the skyline. Webb takes up the story:

> Tupper was running like a hare. It was incredible. Wilson and Tupper rapidly came near. The former was in his long black running costume. Tupper had on shirt and trousers. Both ran in bare feet. Frank and I were equally dumbfounded. We never expected to see Tupper run again. To add to our amazement, when they were about 400 yards away Wilson accelerated and Tupper responded and came with him. Running abreast they sped towards us. Tupper impishly made a short burst when close to us and they reached us together.

Although the selectors refused to relent, Tupper worked his passage to Helsinki as a galley assistant and promptly caused a stir when he beat Finland's Olympic 800 metres contender, who happened to work as a harbour official, in a race along the wharf. Those Olympics were memorable in so many ways, but I digress. This is simply a record of Wilson's determination to restore Tupper to full health, with his usual concoction of fresh air, nuts, berries and freedom proving vital ingredients. The two athletes were kindred spirits in many ways, despite their fundamentally different temperaments.

Wilson's Greatest Day?

THE WORLD RECORD DECATHLON AND ROUTING OF THE 'YANK' GINO FINN.

Wilson's greatest achievement on the athletics track – and certainly the achievement he rated most highly – came in May 1947 in Philadelphia when he competed as a guest in the USA Decathlon Championships and recorded the highest ever points score in that ten-event competition.

Wilson had been enraged by the fact that Don Davis and Rex Myland, two highly promising young British athletes who both hoped to compete in the 1948 London Olympics, had adopted the Gino Finn system of training, as advocated by the successful American decathlete Gino Finn. Wilson, ordinarily a modest and reticent man, was outraged that such renegade American techniques could ruin Britain's top young athletes, and he set out to systematically discredit the 'Yank' by proving the superiority of his own methods.

Wilson's intensely patriotic feelings at this juncture reflected the mood of the nation. Weary, exhausted and half starved after having endured six years of war and the ensuing eighteen months of rationing, envious eyes were being cast westwards towards the 'land of plenty'. Yet again, and against seemingly overwhelming odds, it was a matter of British honour that Wilson should use this opportunity to show the Americans exactly what the Brits could do.

Wilson could be swift in both thought and deed when he was in the mood and, without mentioning his plans to anybody, he booked a costly transatlantic flight at his own expense and arrived quietly in Philadelphia to prepare for the American Decathlon Championships. Frank Ducker got wind of Wilson's plan one morning in the 'foreign news' section of his daily newspaper and, being a bachelor of independent means, moved quickly to book the last seat on that night's flight. His decision was fortuitous, ensuring that the finest moment in Britain's athletics history was witnessed and recorded for posterity by one of his keenest supporters.

Wilson was a man possessed. His most startling performance was a world record of nine seconds flat for the 100 metres; admittedly it was a hand-held timing, but three of the four timekeepers clocked him at nine seconds and only the fourth had him at just a fraction over that. Finn responded by breaking Jesse Owens' world record of 26 feet 9 inches in the long jump but Wilson was only warming up. He answered with a sensational 28 feet, a distance not surpassed until 1968 when Bob Beamon jumped 29 feet 2.2 inches at altitude in Mexico City.

His remaining performances are listed below. Note that in the high jump he cleared 6 feet 7 inches with a backward flip technique almost identical to the revolutionary 'Fosbury Flop' with which Dick Fosbury won the 1968 Olympic championship. His shot, 400 metres, hurdles and discus were very good but not exceptional. However, his javelin throw – which he took left-handed having jarred his right shoulder slightly in the discus – was approaching world record territory, and his 1500 metres time of three minutes forty-five seconds was the fastest ever seen in a multi-event competition.

Using modern-day International Association of Athletics Federations scoring tables I have calculated that Wilson's two-day orgy of athletics excellence would have seen him accumulate 10,012 points, compared with the current world record of Roman Sebrle, from the Czech Republic, who set a mark of 9026 in Gotziz in May 2001. Daley Thompson's best ever mark was 8798 when he won the Olympic Games in Los Angeles in 1984.

The Perfect Ten:
Wilson's individual performances in Philadelphia

Event	Result	IAAF score
100 metres	9.0 seconds	1292
Long jump	28 feet (8.53 metres)	1199
High jump	6 feet 7 inches (2.06 metres)	859
Shot	60 feet (18.25 metres)	991
400 metres	46.0 seconds	1009
110 metres hurdles	13.6 seconds	1027
Discus	170 feet (51.90 metres)	911
Javelin	260 feet (79.25 metres)	1032
Pole vault	15 feet 6 inches(4.72 metres)	825
1500 metres	3 minutes 45 seconds	1067

Total points: 10,012

Existing world decathlon record: Roman Sebrle (Czech Republic). 9026 points (10.64; 8.11m; 2.12m; 15.33m; 47.79; 13.92; 47.92m; 70.16m; 4.80m; 4min 21.95 secs.) Sebrle thus beat Wilson in just three events – high jump, 400 metres and pole vault.

BBC ATHLETICS COMMENTATOR STUART STOREY WRITES:

The Wilson story is all about making dreams come true, the science of rendering the impossible a reality. Commonplace even. When desire, determination, skill and a truly exceptional physiology are in the mix then the outcome must be an exceptional performer. William Wilson is just such a man. For two centuries he has been beaten only once in the competitive arena, and that was in the marathon of 1896 when there were exceptional circumstances, as we read earlier. His appetite for competition is unrivalled, and there is also an obvious relish in breaking records, a healthy but not overbearing ego. The changes in competition implements and event rules in athletics over the years have made no difference to the performances he has achieved. He has always been the best of his era, whatever the era.

It is widely assumed that he must possess the best strength to weight ratio ever recorded, although Loughborough University have not been able to contact him to invite him for tests. But his performances over two centuries have surely given us proof enough about this intensely private man, who shows himself only when he considers it important. Many thought he might return to competition in 2004 for the Athens Olympics (remember he'd won the Marathon in the old stadium in 1938 at the age of 143.) With Jackson, Edwards, Christie and Gunnell all retired the cupboard looked bare for Britain. Then again, we hadn't reckoned on Kelly Holmes. After the poor showing of Britain's athletes at the 2005 World Championships in Helsinki Britain is sorely in need of a hero. I note, with some excitement, that there have recently been reports from the fringes of Axmoor of a spate of sheep hurdles going missing.

With a view to the 2012 Olympics, I believe the decathlon remains the event where his unique talents could be best showcased. A gold medal win would allow us to anoint him officially as the greatest athlete the world has ever seen. I believe he will have kicked on considerably from his world record in Philadelphia in 1947. My BBC colleague Paul Dickinson and I have often constructed a 'Fantasy Decathlon', as all athletics enthusiasts occasionally do, in which Wilson approaches 12,000 points. I know that David Coleman and the the the late Ron Pickering used to play the same game on their travels around the athletics world.

Where can the great man improve for 2012? The high jump definitely. Remember his last competitive jump, in 1947, was still into a sandpit with none of the advantages a soft landing bed offers. A forty-two-second relay leg would suggest the possibility of a forty-three-second run in the 400 metres, a big improvement on his Philadelphia run, while his sensational basic speed would indicate that if he could master the most rudimentary hurdling technique he could knock out a thirteen-dead run. Wilson's discus is poor, though the new smooth two-kilogram weights have seen distances improve in recent decades. I wonder just how much he has ever trained for discus. As for the polevault, his bodyweight ratio makes him a natural and I have no doubt that he would rewrite the record books – again – if let loose with one of the modern-day fibreglass models. It was intriguing to read recent reports that coach Petrov, who guided Sergei Bubka to become the greatest pole vaulter in history, has gone missing from his training base with at least six fibre-glass poles. Finally a three minute forty-eight second mile converts to a three minute thirty second 1500 metres. It would be a big task, at the end of two gruelling days, but I fancy that Wilson would run close.

WILSON'S CLIMB

30 March 1946 – *Wizard* no.1099

Greene, the great athlete, clung on to the rock face and glanced down at me. Then he shifted the rope linking us together and looped it round a projecting spur. 'Right Tom,' he said. 'You can work your way up the face now.' I left the ledge on which I had been standing and started to climb. If my eyebrows had been long enough I should have used them, as well as my fingertips and toes, for the climb was a hard one. But I made it, and stood on the foot-wide ledge which Greene had reached. Above us was another thirty or forty feet of cliff.

Our climb was up Wilson's Climb, in Cumberland. I'm Tom Vale, as you know, and I had been travelling north with Greene to appear in a sports meeting in Glasgow. As we had a day in hand, Greene had suggested breaking our journey for an afternoon in the fresh air, and to attempt the climb of perhaps the most difficult rock face in the district. I've told you much about that strange fellow, ex-Corporal Greene, of the RAF, how we first met in a German prison camp, and how by exercises he had cured my crippled leg. I've told you how, by methods of his own, he had made me so supremely fit that I became a first-class athlete myself.

Greene's own style, and his tremendous physical feats, often reminded the critics of Wilson, the most famous athlete of all time, who was shot down while fighting in the Battle of Britain as a squadron leader. I've told you, too, of the contempt Greene had for awards and prizes. 'Where do we go from here?' I asked as I scanned the cliff. 'I'm not a human fly.' A grin appeared on Greene's thin face. I could tell he was enjoying himself. He had told me already that he had made the climb before. 'Watch how I go,' he said. With the rope hanging loose behind him Greene began to work himself up. His boots hung around his neck as he was climbing barefooted, and he wore his suit of rough homespun tweeds. The fact that there was a fall of at least two hundred feet did not seem to worry him.

He moved up fast fitting his fingers and toes into the tiny cracks and crevices, and in quick time had gained the next ledge. Very slowly, helped all the time by his advice, I got up to where he stood. 'The last twenty feet now,' Greene said, and immediately began to climb again. Greene had told me something about Wilson's climb. It got its name because Wilson was the man who first made the ascent some time in 1846, said local history. I took this to be one of the great athlete's ancestors, for I'd never believed the story that the athlete Wilson of modern times was actually over a hundred and fifty years old, and that his long life and his athletic performances were due to his methods of living. 'Man can be his own master,' Wilson had written not long before he was missing over the channel. 'There is nothing he cannot do if he had the determination to do it. My way of living renews youth.'

Fine words, perhaps, but I could not credit the claim that Wilson, who had been lost in 1940 in the Battle of Britain, was actually born in 1795. Greene quickly accomplished the final 20 feet of the ascent, and a minute later I stood by him and drew a deep breath. I saw Greene stoop and pick up a slab of stone. 'Come on Tom,' he said. 'Everyone who makes the climb adds a stone to the cairn.' I nodded and picked up a stone myself. A little way back from the edge of the cliff was a big pile of stones – quite a monument now to the skill and keenness of British rock climbers. 'Local legend has it that Wilson cleared the space for the cairn and placed the big slab at the bottom,' Greene remarked. We had brought some sandwiches, and ate them in the shadow of the cairn. It was with reluctance that we left the scene, turned our backs on the cliff, and took the easy slope down to the valley. We had a five-mile walk to the station where we caught a local train on to Carlisle. There was only half an hour to wait at Carlisle for the Glasgow train, and so it

was not worthwhile leaving the station. I felt ready to sit down after our day in the open air but as Greene paced up and down the platform I kept in step with him. Presently, with the idea of getting something to read, I turned towards the bookstall.

My glance fixed on a pile of books. On the cover was a photograph of an athlete in full stride. I looked at the title and saw *How to be a Wilson: His Training System in Full* by E. L. Linter. The price of the book was half a crown, and I brought it. Still standing at the bookstall, I read the foreword.

> It is surely the ambition of all young athletes to emulate Wilson, the super runner and jumper whose tragic death during the Battle of Britain put an end to a glorious career. Who among you would not wish to dazzle the crowds as did Wilson, and emblazon your name among the stars of the athlete world? My purpose in writing this book is to provide you with the system which Wilson used, and which, if followed faithfully, will enable you to train into stardom. I knew Wilson intimately, and the system which you will find in this book is just as he told it to me in his heyday. Those of you who have no athletics ambitions will also find his system of great value in the art of keeping fit. – E. L. Linter.

Greene loomed at my elbow. 'What have you got there?' he demanded. I turned the book towards him. The wrinkles round his eyes deepened. He put out his hand and took the volume. As he flicked through the pages I saw there were numerous photographs, evidently taken when Wilson was appearing at sports meetings in pre-war days. 'I'd like to look at this in the train, Tom,' he said harshly. As the train travelled north, Greene sat with the book open in his hands. We had the compartment to ourselves. I said nothing for some time. Greene read the first few pages closely. Then he turned them over rapidly. At last I spoke jokingly. 'Learning anything?' I asked. He looked up and his face was angry.

'Tom, this is a fraud,' he said. 'It's worse than mere nonsense. Any young fellow trying to follow this system could do harm to himself.'

'Is it a fake,' I asked.

'It's deliberately dishonest,' rapped out Greene. 'It's a libel on Wilson. He wouldn't have had anything to do with the stunts in this.'

'The writer must be trying to cash-in on his acquaintance with the great Wilson,' I suggested.

'He never even knew Wilson,' Greene said heatedly. 'The whole thing's a sham, a fake! The system is a mixture of rubbish and lies.'

He passed me the book and I started to look at it. The author, whoever he was, had put his arguments over in a glib fashion. The text was plentifully sprinkled with Wilson's name, and there were lengthy passages in the first person as if Wilson were actually being quoted. But to any expert athlete it was obvious that the whole thing was a fraud. It was cheap, trashy advice that was contained under such chapter headings as 'How Wilson kept a hundred per cent fit', 'How Wilson trained for the mile' and 'How Wilson planned his diet'. Greene, I could tell, was gravely concerned. He sat staring out of the window, but his eyes were not taking in the scenery as the train ran down the upper valley of the Clyde. He was deeply thoughtful and worried.

It was not until we left the train at Glasgow Central that we realised that we had acquaintances on the train. I saw Frank Ducker, the British A.A. official, coming down the platform in company with Captain W.S.K. Webb, now the sporting editor of a London paper and the chief chronicler of Wilson's deeds in pre-war days. We joined them. We had a meal together, when the talk was mostly about the meeting next day. Frank was pleased because there was a really fine entry. However, as soon as the waiter had gone Greene opened out about the book. 'Have you read *How to be a Wilson?*' he demanded, and produced our copy. Frank shook his head and picked up the book. Webb spoke emphatically.

'A copy came to the office for review,' he said. 'I took a look, and then chucked it into the wastepaper-basket.'

'It can't be ignored,' Greene said. 'It's a blot on Wilson's name.'

'Who's the author,' I inquired. Webb was able to give us the information.

'Linter's a shady type,' he said. 'He's a writer who specialises in sensational stuff. The bar's been up against him in our office ever since he sold us an article which he said was by a famous American athlete. We published it in good faith, and then discovered it was faked. I expect he'll be in Glasgow for the sports. He usually turns up at big events.'

Greene evidently heard this with satisfaction. 'I'll make it my business to see him,' he said vigorously. 'He isn't getting away with it.'

•••

LOUDSPEAKER ARGUMENT

Rain had been falling before the start of the sports meeting at Glasgow, and though the skies cleared the ground was sodden. Under the circumstances I was satisfied when I ran the mile in four minutes ten seconds, this giving me an easy pace. Greene received a tremendous reception when he appeared to run in the hundred yards' handicap, for which scores of runners were entered from all the noted harrier clubs of Scotland – Shettleston Harriers, Maryhill, Bellahouston and Dundee Thistle among them. The crowd were surprised by his unimpressive appearance in his black costume, but there was nothing unimpressive about his running. On a day when an even time would have been excellent, he electrified the spectators by clocking nine seconds dead in the final of the race. I handed him his tweed jacket, and he was putting it on when Webb hurried towards us. 'Linter's here,' he said.

'Where is he?' snapped Greene. An astonished exclamation broke from Webb. He pointed to the wooden platform occupied by the announcer in the middle of the arena. 'That's Linter, just going up the ladder,' he said. We were close enough to get a good look at the author of *How to be a Wilson*. He was a tall, florid man in a thick, dark overcoat. He was holding his hat in his hand. The announcer said something to him, and then switched on the microphone. 'Attention, please, ladies and gentlemen,' boomed the loudspeakers. 'Among the many distinguished visitors we have here this afternoon Mr Edelston Linter, whom I now have the pleasure of introducing to you. Mr Linter is a link with the great Wilson.'

Despite the years that had gone since Wilson was shot down, the mention of his name drew applause. 'Mr Linter tells me that he and Wilson knew each other intimately, and that it is upon talks he had with that great athlete that he has based his new book *How to be a Wilson*. I guess you'd like a few words from Mr Linter, so folks, here he is,' concluded the announcer.

Linter waved his hat to all points of the compass as the crowd cheered. 'Thanks, friends!' he said into the microphone. 'I don't want to step between you and the next item on the programme, which I believe is the high jump, but I'd just like to say how pleased I am to be with you this afternoon. The war struck down many sportsmen, but surely athletics had no crueller blow than when Wilson died a hero's death.'

Linter's voice was oily, and I should have liked to have thrown something at him. 'I'm certain of one thing – that if Wilson were still alive he'd be with us this afternoon.' Linter went on. 'Alas, that cannot be, but I thank you for this opportunity of recalling him to your memory. My fuller tribute, and the inside knowledge I gained from that amazing man, is in my little book, *How to be a Wilson*. And so I will say no more now except cheerio and good luck!'

Greene strode swiftly towards the platform. Before Linter could descend he was climbing the ladder. The announcer gave him a hand up, and seemed delighted to be joined by another celebrity. After a brief consultation the announcer again switched on the speakers. 'Greene would like a few words with you,' he said. 'You've just seen him run a cracking hundred yards. Now you'll hear him speak.'

As silence fell Greene spoke into the microphone. 'Some of you may have brought the book *How to be a Wilson*. ' He said harshly. 'For those who've got it, I've two words of advice – burn it!' If Linter had been slapped across the face his smile could not have disappeared quicker. The crowd gasped as the loudspeakers boomed out the words. Greene held out a commanding arm. 'The system it recommends is bad, thoroughly bad,' Greene rasped. 'The so-called exercises are founded on fallacies. Wilson would never have said such utter rubbish, and it's an insult to him to maintain that he did.'

With a shove of his elbow Linter pushed Greene aside, and stood in front of the microphone again. 'This sounds like sour grapes to me,' he sneered.

'No, it's the truth,' snapped Greene. 'I call on you to withdraw the statement that your book is founded on Wilson's methods.'

Linter uttered a laugh. 'I refuse to withdraw a single word,' he said. 'I was honoured by Wilson's friendship, and I regard the book as memorial to him. I stand by what I've written, seeking nothing else but fair play.'

Webb stared at me and shrugged. 'I told you Linter was smart,' he remarked. 'He's swung the crowd his way. He suggested pretty cleverly that Greene's merely jealous.' Webb was right. I detected cat-calls and jeers as Greene turned away and started to come down the ladder.

'Strikes me Greene advertised the book instead of condemning it,' I said. Greene returned towards us his face expressionless. 'You were a bit impulsive, old chap,' Webb said. 'I warned you Linter was a slippery customer to tackle.'

Greene may have realised his error, for the loudspeaker argument would be reported in every newspaper in the country – but he made no allusion to what had happened. His glance fixed on Webb.

'I'd be grateful if you could arrange for a party of officials and newspaper reporters to meet me at Wilson's Climb at noon on Monday,' he said.

'Wilson's Climb? Oh, you mean that rock face in Cumberland,' Webb exclaimed. 'Yes, I'll fix it,' I caught the note of excitement in his voice. 'Gosh, I'll have them all there.'

'Thanks!' Greene said. 'I'd like Linter to be there as well.'

•••

THE BIG SURPRISE

I stayed with friends in Glasgow over the weekend, and travelled to Cumberland with Frank Ducker and Captain Webb on the Monday morning. Linter was on the train, and a large party of reporters from Scottish newspapers were also making the journey. There was an advertisement in my paper for *How to be a Wilson* and the announcement stated that 50,000 copies had been sold. I remarked on this to Webb, and he commented. '50,000 suckers.'

When we reached the little country station we found the local bus proprietor waiting with his vehicle. He was sure of good business. The driver, near whom I was seated, could not hurry along the rough moorland tracks, and we had to survive some heavy jolts and bumps in the course of the journey. I observed from my knowledge of the district that he was taking the longer route to bring us up the easier slope to the top of the escarpment. I mentioned this to him, and he replied that Mr Greene had instructed him to take the visitors up to the cairn. 'Not that I shall get right there,' he added. 'They'll have to walk the last half-mile.'

We could see the cairn sticking up on the skyline when we got out of the bus and straggled across the rough turf. A chill breeze was blowing, and there was a hint of rain in the clouds piling up to the west. I heard more than one grumble. Some of the reporters evidently considered they were on some form of wild goose chase, and this idea was strengthened when we reached the top and there was no sign of Greene. Linter uttered a sarcastic laugh. 'I doubt if you will see him,' he remarked. 'It looks like a hoax to me.'

A faint hail reached our ears. I stepped to the edge of the cliff. At the foot of Wilson's climb two hundred feet below, stood Greene in his running costume, his feet bare, hands cupped over his mouth he called to us.

'I want you to time me, Frank,' he shouted. 'When you're ready, give me the word.'

'Okay, Greene!' Frank replied and wound up his stopwatch. Several members of the party apparently had no head for heights, and had to keep away from the edge, but most of us stood on the brink and stared down at the tiny figure far below. Frank shouted 'Go!' and started the watch ticking.

We saw Greene spring forward. At our distance he looked like a fly on a wall. A bulging fold hid him. A few instants passed, and he came up from beneath it, and without a second's respite, tackled the next steep, forbidding section. From my own climb I could appreciate the tremendous physical energy that the sustained effort demanded. Greene was coming up the last stretch now and the strain was visible on his face. Thrusting, pulling, balancing, he neared the top, pushed his arms over the edge, and levered himself over on to the level ground where we were standing.

Frank had a raincoat, which he threw over Greene's sweating shoulders, and even those doubting pressmen raised a cheer.

'What was the time?' he gasped breathlessly.

'It's unbelievable,' Frank exclaimed. 'Three minutes.'

Greene gave a deep sigh of satisfaction. 'I've another thing to ask now,' he said. 'Will you help me to remove the stones from the cairn?'

There were murmurs of protest, but Webb walked straight to the cairn and began to pull down the stones. Soon several of us were helping. Gradually the site of the pile dwindled as we demolished the cairn. I remember the growing air of excitement as we pulled the last few stones away. We looked down at the flat slab a couple of feet square perhaps, with square edges.

'If legend be true this is the stone laid by Wilson after his climb a hundred years ago,' I said. Greene was the focus of keen attention as he stooped, got his fingers under the stone, lifted it and dropped it aside. He stooped again, put his hand into a hole, and pulled out an object so dirt-encrusted that it was difficult to recognise it as a bottle. With a sharp tap he smashed it on a stone, and from the fragments took out a roll of paper.

There was a rush to get near as he carefully unrolled the paper. In the act of unrolling it he gazed round at us. 'I will repeat from memory what is written on the paper,' he said in a harsh, undramatic voice. 'It says: On the fifth day of March in the year eighteen hundred and forty-six William Wilson climbed the big rock in three minutes. In witness to which we set our names, George Garth, gentleman, Edmund Kemp, farmer.'

The hush was broken by Webb, who was gazing at the document. 'This is just what it says,' he said jerkily. 'Word for word.'

'Will you turn over and read what is there?' Greene asked.

Webb's hands shook as he turned the paper over.

'Immediately after performing the climb William Wilson descended the big rock in one minute,' he read out. 'In witness to which …'

'Look out!' shouted Manton. 'Stop him!'

Greene sprang forward. For an instant we saw him poised on the edge of the cliff. Then he vanished with a leap into space. He had not made a suicide jump. I saw him plunge down close to the cliff face, saw his feet touch for an instant on a six-inch ledge, and saw him leap again. He landed on the bulge I mentioned before and took off again, dropping with his arms held close to his sides, and legs together, until he landed on another ledge, from which, with scarcely a pause, he jumped again. With our hearts in our mouths we watched him. But no one spoke. From the physical point of view alone, forgetting the courage required, the time and judgment required when the slightest error could mean death, were amazing. With a final bound he reached the base of the cliff. A long pent-up sigh exploded from us.

'I knew it! I knew it!' gasped Webb. 'I've always thought so, and this is the proof.'

Somebody called out that Greene was climbing up again. This time he did not exhibit the same frantic haste but none the less it was a swift ascent. I was the first to grasp his arm as he came over the top. 'Well, there it is!' he said, with a shrug.

Webb's mouth opened in a hoarse shout. 'Wilson!' he cried. 'Wilson!'

The man I had known so long as Greene folded his arms. 'My second identity suited very well,' he said. 'I'd hoped to keep it. I should have kept it but for that man.' He turned and fixed his gaze on Linter. 'So I had to prove who I really am to vindicate myself and expose a fraud.'

'Wilson alive!' Manton exclaimed. 'Gosh, it'll be a world sensation.' He whirled round on Linter. 'What have you got to say for yourself man?'

Linter had nothing to say. His high colouring had gone, and he looked pasty. He passed the tip of his tongue over his dry lips muttered something, turned away, and stumbled off.

Wilson smiled thinly. 'I'm sorry to have been melodramatic, but I could think of no other way to give you certain proof of my identity,' he said.

'When I was shot down over the Channel I managed to swim ashore. In the course of the swim I had to discard most of my clothing, and when I was taken prisoner I found the Germans thought I was a member of a bomber crew which had been shot down. I thought it was a good opportunity to lose my identity. Wilson had become too famous. It worried me. I sought to disappear, and, shall we say, start again in the obscurity I prefer. But I don't seem able to steer clear of the limelight.'

I remember how eager the pressmen were to get away to the nearest phone and tell the world that Wilson was alive. We let them go. Wilson, Ducker, Webb, and myself let them use the bus while we walked. 'I'd never meant to appear in athletics again,' Wilson said as we went along. 'Then I met Tom Vale, and recognised in him the raw material. Sorry to describe you as raw material, Tom.'

'I know just how raw,' I chuckled.

'The raw material for building into athletic greatness,' Wilson said. He smiled. 'In bringing Tom along I again achieved a certain fame, and our partnership isn't over yet – in fact, it may hardly have begun.'

GILBERT LAWFORD DALTON

IT is very difficult, off hand, to think of two comic book hero characters more different than Wilson of the *Wizard* and Alf Tupper, the 'Tough of the Track'. One is the mystical athlete from the Moor, with something of the supernatural about him, a food faddist and fanatic: an athlete to appeal to the aesthete. The other is the grimy welder from Greystone who between races gorged himself on fish and chips. Almost the only thing they share is their legendary status. Except that both, remarkably, were penned by the same hand.

The chances are that you have never heard of Gilbert Lawford Dalton, but any British male over the age of 50 will certainly have read him. He is, almost certainly, the most prolific author in the history of the English language: throughout his working life he averaged over a million words *a year*. In his own way he was just as much of a sporting superman as William Wilson himself.

Not only did Dalton bash out Wilson and Tough of the Track – 5000 words a time on a weekly basis – but he is also known to have been the unseen hand penning 'I Flew with Braddock', 'Braddock VC', 'Goals that Count', 'Wonderman', 'Cannonball Kid', 'Tom Smith', 'Fielding that Counts', 'Baldy Hogan', 'Red Rocket', 'It's Cricket' and 'Tom Smith's Schooldays'.

In one six-week period in 1949 Dalton wrote - because he had to - 316,000 words of serial fiction, one novel of 80,000 words, and three episodes of a radio serial. Time was , as you can imagine, always tight. A 5000-word Wilson story he considered a mere morning's work. His personal best for such an assignment was 2 hours 33 minutes.

Born in 1903, a journalist by training and inclination, Dalton worked before the War as *The Times*'s stringer in Coventry and as a sports freelance covering cricket, football and athletics for the *Daily Telegraph*. It was during the Second World War, prevented from serving by his chronic asthma, that he moved away from papers and became a full-time in-house writer for the D. C. Thomson organisation who produced such comics as the *Wizard*. The in-house writers worked in collaboration with their Editor-in-Chief William Blain, who had an extraordinary imagination and sewed the seeds for many of the characters. He would advise and guide, but ultimately it was Dalton who produced. At one stage Blain wrote to Dalton that he wanted 'a series on the supreme athlete, a man who would be named Wilson. A winner but a man who was as unassuming as he was mysterious.' We can see the hand of Blain again in the genesis of Alf Tupper in a note he wrote to Dalton in August 1948 lamenting Britain's poor performance in the 1948 Olympics in London:

I believe that the sight of real world form will cause a great revival of interest in athletics, as happened after

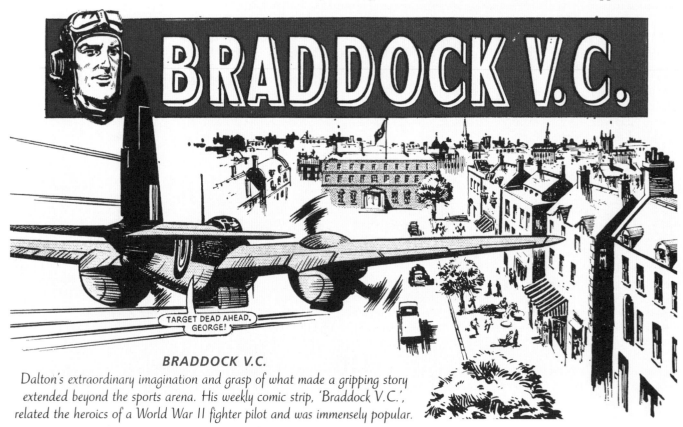

BRADDOCK V.C.

Dalton's extraordinary imagination and grasp of what made a gripping story extended beyond the sports arena. His weekly comic strip, 'Braddock V.C.', related the heroics of a World War II fighter pilot and was immensely popular.

1908 with Applegarth, Albert Hill and such people coming on. I've a notion for an athletics story next summer but it can wait. One good result that will come from the Olympic failure by Britain will be the clearing out of the columns of some over-publicised names. A proper sense of values and critical standards may now be allowed to develop.

Dalton evidently possessed an incredible magpie-like brain, collecting and then storing every little detail and anecdote for some indefinite moment in the future when he would unveil it in print, often in some slightly modified form. This is a man who in the modern era would probably be the World Trivial Pursuit champion. A brief scroll through his journal – part diary, part musings and jottings to himself - reveals an extraordinary eclectic mind:

17 September 1946: Simonides's epitaph to the dead at Thermopylae: 'Go tell the Spartans, thou that passest by. That here obedient to their laws we lie.'

7 October 1946: Talking to stranger on the train to Dundee who, it transpires, is a motorcyclist: 'Have you ever competed in the Manx TT?' I asked. "I have won it," replied the stranger. I learn that he was Ernie Lyons, an Irishman, and he said he found the four ascents of Shelsby Walsh a greater strain than the TT. A motorcyclist, during a race, is constantly listening to his engine.

28 December 1946: Clash of film titles (double billings): *A Fig Leaf for Eve – Something for the Boys*; *They Met in the Dark – Behind Closed Doors*; *The Man Who Dared - Lost in a Harem*; *That Night with You - Born for Trouble*.

30 January 1947: H. de Vere Stackpole: 'A turnip has only oneself. A man is different. An imaginative man is very different. He is often in fact a crowd and a very mixed crowd.'

27 October 1947: [A cutting from a newspaper takes his eye.] To actress who has just had a baby boy: 'Don't call him Robert. Robert's such a common name. Every Tom, Dick and Harry is called Robert!'

2 December 1948: A point that may be useful in a detective yarn is that a Chinese can be distinguished from a Jap by the way they chew sunflower seeds. The Chinese uses his lips, the Jap his teeth.

6 March 1949: From Bill Edrich's book on cricket: Andy Ducat died while batting at Lord's. Three nights in succession he had dreamed that William Beldham, the old Surrey player whose portrait hangs at Lord's in top-hat and smock, had beckoned to him. In 1944 at Lord's, Bob Wyatt (RAF) was bowling to Jack Robertson (Army) when a V-1 came over in a shallow dive. It exploded 300 yards away. Wyatt scrambled up and resumed his bowling and Robertson hit him for six.

Occasionally Dalton founds time to ponder on his prodigious productivity – a million words a year is a conservative estimate for when he was in his pomp – and on whence he drew his inspiration.

14 December 1947: How do I get my ideas? I suppose I am gifted with a 'teeming brain' stoked by memory and the books I read and the impressions that impinge as I travel about. Into my mind now comes a scene in a chemist's shop to start the broadcast play *The Casting Vote* I am writing. The chemist of course is a member of the UDC and the shop a rendezvous for his fellow councillors. This undeniably a flashback to my childhood when my father – then a journalist – would call daily at Mr Westman's shop in Kidderminster (I still remember the huge coloured bottles) to pick up gossip. The subconscious seems to be an inexhaustible well for ideas. I wonder if one ever really forgets anything.

24 January 1948: It is often suggested that high speed produces bad work, and that may clearly be so sometimes. But generally speaking, in my experience, the exact reverse is the case. The man working against time produces better work than the man who hasn't much to do and can take as long as he likes. In other words the overworked man produces better quality results than the underworked man.

Occasionally it does all seem to get too much for Dalton. Remember these are harsh times with the euphoria of winning the war giving way to the grim reality of a Britain in ruins as a result of its heroic efforts:

August 27 1947: Announcement that Basic Petrol ceases on 1 October. As all the things that make life worth living are taken from us one by one the phrase of Keats, 'and for many a time I have been half in love with easeful death', keeps occurring. This is bleak pessimism but two major wars in a lifetime and the suspense of crisis after crisis must have an abrasive effect upon one's resilience . . .

Dalton died in Weymouth Hospital on 28 March 1963, unrecognised by the world he had helped, in a considerable way, to foster. Written on the inside cover of both his surviving log books is a short phrase of G.K. Chesterton's about boy's stories: 'the actual centre of a million flaming imaginations'.

It should have been the epitaph carved on Dalton's headstone.

The Perfect Fish and Chips?

LIST OF INGREDIENTS

For the chips:
2 lb Fresh Potatoes, peeled

For the fish:
6 Fresh Haddock Fillets,
  skinned
Plain White Flour
1/8 tsp Salt
1/8 tsp Ground White Pepper
1 lemon

For the batter:
8 oz Plain White Flour
1/2 tsp Salt
2 tbs Sunflower Oil
2 x Eggs, separated
6 tbsp Water

1 pint Sunflower Oil,
  for deep frying

INSTRUCTIONS FOR PREPARATION

Peel the potatoes and cut into chips, the size being to your liking. Soak them in cold water for 30 minutes.

Wipe the fish and lightly coat with a little seasoned flour. To make the best batter, sift flour and salt into a bowl before separating the two eggs. Then add yolks, oil and water and beat vigorously until a smooth consistency is achieved.

Heat oil in a deep fryer to 360°F/ 180°C. Drain the chips and dry well before putting carefully into the oil. Fry, in batches, for 4-5 minutes till tender but not brown. Remove and drain on kitchen paper to remove excess oil.

Reduce the temperature of the oil to 340°F /170°C. Whisk the egg whites till stiff but not dry, and fold into the batter. Coat the fish with batter. Fry the fish, one at a time if necessary, for 2 to 3 minutes each side till crisp and golden. Drain on kitchen paper and keep hot, uncovered.

Increase the temperature of the oil to 360°F /180°C again, put the chips in the basket and fry till crisp and golden. Drain on kitchen paper and pile into a warmed serving dish.

Garnish the fish with lemon wedges and sprigs of parsley. Serve immediately.

Calories: 114   Calories from fat: 73

Daily Values:

Total Fat 81.2g (125%)   Carbohydrate 57.9g (19%)
Saturated Fat 8.5g (42%)   Dietary Fibre 3.9g (16%)
Cholesterol 180mg (60%)   Protein 46.6g
Sodium 441mg (18%)

CONCLUSION

Fish and chips is high in fat and should only be consumed on large 'industrial' scale by elite athletes or heavy manual labourers who can convert that fat instantly into energy. The addition of mushy peas is highly advisable, some sort of greens being desirable, as well as helping with the fibre intake.

Fish and chips was, and still is, a relatively cheap meal and in that respect was perfect for the young Tupper. It also served as his comfort food, and its value should not be underestimated in that respect. It lifted his morale when he was feeling low, and it was as much a 'reward' as it was his basic fuel.

ALF TUPPER – LONE WOLF RUNNER

> SPIKES, EH? YOU'RE A RUNNER, THEN?

> YES, I'M GOING TO NORTHCASTLE TO RUN AT CITY PARK TOMORROW. I WANT TO RUN AGAINST HAROLD PILKINGTON IN THE MILE.

-Alf Tupper – the 'Tough of the Track' to generations of British schoolboys and athletics fans – was Wilson's antithesis. He was a 'common man' made good, as opposed to a 'superman' doing what he had to do. While Wilson spent his illustrious life pushing the human body to hitherto unimagined extremes, breaking world records on an apparently weekly basis, climbing overhanging rock faces, and shooting down Germans by the score in his Spitfire, Tupper's main achievement was simply to flourish against overwhelming odds. There were a couple of Olympic gold medals separated by forty years – the first in the mile at the Helsinki Olympics in 1952 and the second in the 1500 metres in Barcelona in 1992 – and he also claimed a world mile record in 1968. But in general Alf's great appeal was more mundane and anecdotal than purely extreme physical achievement; indeed his wins and triumphs are often modest, almost unrecorded affairs. His colourful language – 'I ran 'em all'. 'Bloomin' ada' and 'lummy' helped endear Alf to his reading public and quickly moved into common usage.

He always battled the odds, and was the eternal gutter-snipe waging war against the toffs and scoundrels who seemed to populate the British and European athletics circuit, a fight which he also carried into everyday life when the odds seemed stacked against him.

As such he still enjoys cult hero status with athletes of the calibre of Ron Hill, Brendan Foster, Steve Ovett and, rather more bizarrely, former British shot put champion Geoff Capes all nominating him as their earliest sporting idol. Meanwhile, Leeds University Cross Country Club have named their club after him and regularly pay homage to the great man with fish and chip suppers. Tony Little, of the heavy metal band Iron Maiden, even wrote a song in his honour, 'The Loneliness of the Long Distance Runner' – a panegyric to the Tough of the Track, with the wind and the rain beating down upon him, trying so hard the pulse of his blood is ringing in his head, running till he drops, such is his determination to win…

Alhough he enjoyed an extraordinarily long athletics career – it is unfair to compare anybody with the ageless Wilson in that respect – Tupper did at least have the grace to age a little before our eyes. In his latter years he bore the appearance of a craggy middle-aged boxer who has seen better years, while in the decades before he had morphed from a blonde, clean-cut, fresh-faced boy into the stroppy, spiky-haired, acne-ridden teenager and young man we loved best.

Although they were very different characters, Alf shared Wilson's spartan habits, more out of necessity than choice, having emerged from the scrapheaps and bombsites of post-war Britain to make a virtue of his poverty and tough upbringing. Life was unremittingly grim and harsh, and it never seemed to improve in spite of the fact that Alf

THE SPOILS OF VICTORY

Alf won more than his fair share of vases and cutlery services over the years.

LIFE WAS UNREMITTINGLY GRIM

Alf shared Wilson's Spartan habits, though more out of necessity than choice, having emerged from the scrap-heaps and bomb sites of post-war Britain to make a virtue of his poverty and tough upbringing.

A WILLING WORKHORSE

Alf always found a way of getting the job done, even when it clashed with a big race at the White City on a Saturday.

regularly walked away from the endless succession of 'open' sports meetings he attended around the country with prizes of cutlery and crockery sets. Just getting to these 'meets' was always an adventure for Alf, invariably involving a hitched ride with some dodgy character, or travelling fourth class on a train and having to sleep on the overhanging luggage racks. There was always at least one hapless citizen to save and one dastardly crook to outwit.

Despite the success and honour that came his way, Alf seemed to live in a state of permanent destitution, and remained remarkably positive and good-humoured nonetheless, which no doubt goes a long way towards explaining his popularity. His attitude was one which seemed to say 'Life could be much worse', and in that respect he was very much a man of his time. He set out on life's journey in 1949 when the euphoria of victory in the Second World War had long died down to be replaced by the reality of rationing and unemployment in a society where class still held sway. It is perhaps no coincidence that 1949 was also the year that Evelyn Waugh penned *Brideshead Revisited*, his tale of indulgent youth and privilege going to wasteful and disgraceful pot.

Alf definitely saw himself as an urban street fighter in the class battle that was being waged in post-war England. He liked to be known as the 'Lone Wolf' runner – though in fairness that originally came about because it was the slogan that adorned the only running vest he could afford from the second-hand shop – and frankly gloried a little in his working class background. There should, however, be no doubting that his determination to 'beat the toffs' and 'run 'em all' was a huge motivating factor. His stance was fully understandable in the early years, though it seemed a little outdated by the late eighties and early nineties. Essentially he was the world's great underdog, and the British love an underdog, a small bolshy chap with a chip on both shoulders and a host of points to prove.

THE TOUGH OF THE TRACK

ALWAYS AT LEAST ONE HAPLESS CITIZEN TO SAVE AND DASTARDLY CROOK TO OUTWIT

Perish the thought, but Alf should have been a policeman. He was always on the case, rescuing law-abiding citizens who found themselves in trouble and chasing down crooks who were up to no good.

Alf was a nutritionist's nightmare and surely played a large part in fostering disastrous eating habits in the youth of post-war Britain. In the world of Alf Tupper it is possible to feast on fish and chips, nosh bangers and mash, eat large slabs of cake, drink steaming mugs of sweet tea and *still* run like the wind and smash records. Generations of admiring males happily ate to their heart's content but forgot the running part of the Tupper equation.

His hometown of Greystone was a great, decaying industrial port somewhere 'up north' where he lived his life in an almost Dickensian setting – spartan and joyless. The underlying certainty that Alf and the good guys would always win through was reassuring, though, and took the edge off our anxieties. Leafing through his exploits was like comfort reading. Alf always won through, no matter what the machinations of his cheating opponents, no matter what his downright bad luck.

Life was uncomplicated in a fashion we wouldn't recognize these days. Women just don't feature – the emotional turmoil of relationships, marriage, kids or divorce simply

ALF'S LIFE WAS FULL OF CHEATING OPPONENTS

Somebody was always trying to beat him by foul means rather than fair – whether by jumping the gun, sabotaging his bike or sending him sprawling into the river.

never enters the story. He was a man of his times in that respect. Sex and emotional turmoil were not to be acknowledged or spoken about. His generation had fought and come through a war and there were other things for young men to be worrying about.

Alf was also noted for never getting his just reward. He was invariably cheated out of the prize and glory; his records were always invalid for some reason. It was a constant theme in his life, and again that kept him in tune with much of post-war Britain. The British had played a major part in winning the war and had made huge sacrifices in the process, but they were also left feeling as though they were paying the cost while the 'bad guys' ended up winning.

THE EARLY DAYS

30 April 1949 marks our first encounter with Alf Tupper, though the wavy-haired, blond and blue-eyed youngster whose great deeds were reported with enthusiasm in the

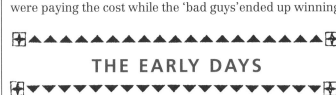

BUT HE ALSO MADE FRIENDS

Kind hearts and coronets. On this occasion an exhausted Alf, having worked through the night before his big race, was given a lift home by his local ice cream seller.

TEN SECONDS! MIND YOU TIMING ON THE GUN FLASH IS A BIT ROUGH AND READY.

WHEW, THAT'S A FAST TIME, BERT. HAVEN'T YOU TWIGGED WHO HE IS? THAT'S ALF TUPPER!

ALF TUPPER! I DIDN'T KNOW HE WAS A SPRINTER. GOING TO SAY ANYTHING TO HIM?

NO. BUT WE'D BETTER TELL FRANK MUDGE ABOUT HIM.

WELL RUN, KID. COME INTO THE HOUSE AND HAVE A BIT OF COLD PORK AND PICKLES FOR SUPPER.

COLD PORK AND PICKLES! LEAD ME TO IT, MISTER.

That night Alf mentioned his towpath experience to Horace Greene, his newsagent pal . . .

NO DOUBT ABOUT IT, ALF YOU STUMBLED ON BLOKES REHEARSING FOR THE BIG PROFESSIONAL SPRINT RACES. ARTHUR MOSS, THE LANDLORD OF THE WHARF INN, HAS ALWAYS BEEN INTERESTED IN THE PRO RACES BUT FRANK MUDGE IS THE BIG NAME AROUND HERE. HE'S THE BIGGEST BUTCHER IN TOWN, BUT HE MAKES MORE OUT OF THE SPRINTS.

HOW DOES HE MANAGE THAT?

BETTING! THEY TRAIN A BLOKE UP, GET HIM A GOOD START, THEN BET ON HIM AND CLEAN UP. IT'S A RACKET.

SO THAT'S WHY THEY WERE TRAINING IN THAT QUIET SPOT. THE PICK OF THE TWO I RAN WAS A BLOKE CALLED MARTIN.

AH, THAT WOULD BE MARTIN JONES. HE'S ONE OF FRANK MUDGE'S RUNNERS. I SAW HIM RUN AT A PROFESSIONAL SPRINT MEETING ONCE. HE WON A PACKET FOR FRANK MUDGE THAT DAY.

NO WONDER THEY LOOKED A BIT PUT OUT WHEN I DID WHAT I SAID, AND BEAT THE BOTH OF 'EM.

Next day, Ike, who was not working because of a cold, turned up at the workshop.

YOU NOT READY TO START WORK YET, IKE?

I'M NOT UP TO WORKING YET, ALF.

IT WOULDN'T DO YOU ANY HARM TO TRY.

NO, I'M STILL UNDER DOCTOR'S ORDERS. HERE'S A LETTER FOR YOU, ALF.

Dear Sir,
I return herewith the postal order for five shillings sent as entry fee for the mile open scratch race at the above sports.
The entry is restricted to members of affiliated clubs and, as you describe yourself as unattached, your entry cannot be accepted.
Yours faithfully,
A. Trouncer,
Hon. Secy.

THEY'VE TURNED ME DOWN FOR THE CAMMERFORD SPORTS. JUST BECAUSE I DON'T BELONG TO A CLUB.

WELL, AT LEAST YOU'VE GOT YOUR MONEY BACK, I ALWAYS RECKONED YOU SPENT TOO MUCH ON YOUR RUNNING.

BETTER SPENDING IT ON MY RUNNING THAN ON THE DOGS THE WAY YOU DO. HERE, IKE, HOW ABOUT SPRINGING ME A FEW EXTRA BOB THIS WEEK? MY BOOTS NEED MENDING.

I'LL SEE WHAT I CAN DO, ALF. HEY, HERE'S FRANK MUDGE. WHAT DOES HE WANT?

18-10-69

Rover bore little resemblance to the grubby street fighter we encountered in the *Victor* in later years.

As with William Wilson there are still a number of holes in Alf's life history, though he is not quite the man of mystery Wilson was. It appears that he was born at sea on a merchant vessel just off the coast of the island of Tristan in the Tristan da Cunha group in the South Atlantic Ocean. The island is notable for being the most remote spot to be inhabited on planet earth, with some 150 souls residing in the island's main settlement of Edinburgh. It is situated some 1600 miles south of St Helena and 1700 miles west of Cape Town. We know this from the episode in which Alf, having fallen out with the England selectors yet again, thumbed his way up to Edinburgh, Scotland, to attend the 1986 Commonwealth Games, where it emerged he was in fact eligible to compete for Tristan Da Cunha – which he promptly did. This is also the famous occasion on which, finding the soft bedding in his bed and breakfast accommodation not to his liking, he remedied the situation by running up Arthur's Seat to sleep on the craggy outcrop there instead.

But we digress. Alf was born into a seafaring family but, alas, was orphaned at an early age. His father went down along with the rest of his ship's crew one fatally stormy night; and his mother failed to survive a tragic house fire when young Alf was just five. Pure Dickens, as was his lonely journey through various orphanages until, at the age of twelve, he was sent to an 'industrial school' called Thorn House, when a magistrate decided that he was in need of proper 'care and upbringing'.

Discipline problems immediately arose at Thorn House due to the headmaster's view that pupils should be given total freedom, which was all very liberal but meant that Alf quickly fell foul of the school bully Butch Harden and his gang. In one episode, a rooftop protest by Butch caused the Head to sack the only member of staff who had been encouraging Alf by giving him welding lessons and nurturing his running talents. Then Alf, always the victim, was punished for fighting after being set upon by Harden and his gang. He was banned from running and welding for six months and reacted predictably by shimmying down a drainpipe one night and running away.

Alf was next spotted a year later when the local council sent him to a summer camp at Bellfield Castle – a gesture he interpreted as charity and therefore only reluctantly participated in the team games, using all his spare time to improve his running.

While there, two 'yobs' – Alf's world was very black and white – taunted him as he easily won the Schoolboy's Mile. Spurred on by their jeers, he decided to run in the Open Mile, for a first prize of a huge haunch of ham. Just before they set off, Alf learned that the yobs had teamed up in a deliberate attempt to thwart the local race veteran, Mr Harland, from winning by 'nudging' him off the track. Angered, Alf decided to tuck in behind the pair and, with a terrific finishing burst, he came through to win the race.

A South American tribe on the banks of the Orinoco River exist on river mud which they bake in the sun. It is then mixed into a paste and eaten.

A favourite Tibetan meal is buttered tea, of which they drink dozens of cups per day.

In 1938 a group of scientists enjoyed steaks from the flesh of a Mammoth which had been preserved for over 20,000 years in the ice caps of Russia.

Dr Fuljames has put Alf on a diet which has been scientifically planned to give him more energy and stamina.

ALF LEFT NO STONE UNTURNED TRYING TO IMPROVE

In his early career Alf scoured books and magazines for advice on diet and nutrition for a budding young athlete. He tried everything but eventually settled for his much loved fish and chips. Note the blond public school look of his teenage years!

YOU DON'T MESS WITH ALF!

Alf worked on the theory that, when faced with a difficult individual, you must get your retaliation in first.
Though normally in the right, he gained the reputation of being 'difficult'.

As for the ham? He donated that to old Harland so that he could continue his annual tradition of offering it to the local old folks home, thus allowing Alf to call it quits with the local council for paying for his place at the camp. This little tale introduces many of Alf's character traits and themes that will recur in his adventures.

We next encounter him in his late teens living with his mean old miserable Aunt Meg in a small one-up-one-down in Anchor Alley where the wallpaper peeled from the walls and the ceiling dripped with condensation. As he recalled some years later: 'Aunt Meg was a big brawny woman with her hair hanging over her red, bad tempered face. She took in washing and the continuous steam in the air kept the peeling walls running with water. For supper she took half a loaf and a greasy package of marge from the cupboard and put them down on the newspaper that served as a tablecloth.'

Anchor Alley was squalid and unlit, 'the darkness broken

Alf sleeps on a mattress on the floor of the damp, airless welding shop.

For twenty-five shillings a week, he works hard all day as a welder.

In the evening, in all kinds of weather, he can be found on a training run through the murky streets of Greystone.

Alf's favourite meal is a fish-and-chip supper, which he has in the evening—when he can afford it.

A DAY IN THE LIFE OF . . .

Sometimes life was very simple for Alf: a good night's sleep, a hard day's work, an equally hard run around
the streets of Greystone every evening and delicious fish and chips every night.

ON THE ROAD

But life could also be hard and depressing – getting evicted from railway huts, thumbing a lift at night or sometimes just putting his head down and trekking to his next destination.

only by a bright light shining through one of the windows where there was the enticing smell of fish and chips from Mrs Spicer's shop.' Bert Bivens, as usual, was ordering his evening meal. It seemed to be an oasis of warmth and civility. No wonder Alf became so keen on fish and chips. It wasn't just sustenance they provided, but also reassurance.

Alf only earned £1 5s. at Ike Smith's where he worked as an apprentice welder under the first arch of the viaduct and Aunt Meg claimed all but 2s. 6d. of that for board and lodging despite the fact there was never any food in the place. We later learned that most of the money went to feed her alcohol addiction – her regular 'stout sessions' with her neighbour Mrs Bow were apparently Aunt Meg's only solace in life. There were occasional bizarre rumours that she had also formed a romantic attachment to Ike, which might possibly explain his chronic lumbago and persistent bad back.

The last straw came very quickly when she stole the 7s. 6d. that Alf had been tipped for mending the exhaust pipe of a passing toff in record time, to stock her larder with bottles of stout. On top of this, she had also pawned the stainless steel cutlery set he had won at the Watbury

Games, his first toe in the water as far as athletics were concerned. She was a dreadful woman in all respects, and Alf finally snapped. 'I'm leaving, I'm finished here. I'll look after myself,' shouted Alf as he threw his few pitiful belongings onto his mattress, rolled them up and marched out of the door forever, with Aunt Meg's screams of abuse echoing all the way down Anchor Valley. It was Alf against the world now.

Alf's first port of call was Horace Greene the newsagent, a kindly man who loved his athletics and used to turn a blind eye when Alf pulled the *Athletics News* down from the shelf and spent the best part of a bitterly cold afternoon reading it. Fred used to tell him tales of Jesse Owens the great American sprinter and jumper who won four medals at the 1936 Olympics.

Another haven was Sam Kessick's café, where the heating was always on full blast in the winter and he could curl up next to the radiator. Apart from his beloved fish and chips – which Sam took good care to wrap up in the sports pages so Alf could read the latest athletics news – Alf used to eat fishpaste sandwiches, bangers and mash, and occasionally, as a treat, stewed eel pie, for all of which

Before World War One there had been an annual fell race from the top of Beacon Hill to Hag's Dyke via the craggy slopes of Gibbet Hill: just over two miles across some extremely rough terrain. The best official time was 15 minutes 30 seconds by Bill Gale in 1914, but local lore had it that back in 1905 Jem Sheppard, a legendary Cumberland Fell runner, had covered the distance in exactly twelve minutes.

A lively debate in the local press pitted Sheppard's grandson against hordes of sceptics led by Mr Walden-Griffiths, a local entrepreneur and racehorse owner, whose explanation of Sheppard's freakishly quick time noted how the race was always timed from the four clock faces on the tower of Hillbury Church, whose times quite often differed from one another by as much as two or three minutes. Walden-Griffiths put up £50 for the first runner who could complete the challenge in 12 minutes. When the crack Granton Hall squad took up the challenge, and the respected runner Noel Evans managed to knock an impressive twenty seconds off the official record, this appeared to be sufficient refutation of Sheppard's claims.

But soon Alf was having a go at the record himself. Lem Saull, who ran the local boxing gym on the first floor of an old warehouse in Wharf Street, had worked wonders in getting him fully fit after a painful rib injury had baffled the medical boffins, but now a raid by Health and Safety officers had closed him down until he could strengthen the gym's floor, which would cost at least £40. Alf always paid his debts. But how to get your hands on such a large sum of money...?

He trained like a dervish for a month, and brought his best time down from fifteen minutes to thirteen. But Alf was still a minute shy of the alleged record. It seemed impossible. At which point Lem Saull observed that Alf wasn't warming up properly, and should loosen up with an hour's fast walking beforehand – just like the steady road work he advised his boxers to do.

The rest is hysteria. Racing with Evans on the appointed day, with Commander Churcher from Granton Hall installed as time-keeper, Alf tore away and took a commanding lead up Gibbet Hill, ascending with a steady zigzag rather than attempting to run straight up its steep slopes. He flogged himself like never before and, making a huge effort to relax despite the fatigue, he let gravity take over for the ascent to Hag's Dyke and ran quicker than he thought possible. The time? 12 minutes exactly.

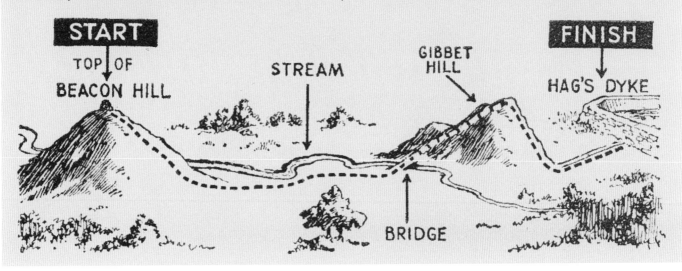

The Strange Case of Running Against W.H. Oami

The prestigious Barlow Cup Individual Cross Country championship had been abandoned mid-race when a blizzard swept over the remote moorland course. Alf, up in front and unawares, had ploughed on, but was surprised to find a long-haired, ponytailed runner tracking him all the way before trailing off 100 yards before the finish – where all the other runners were safely inside the race tent wrapped in blankets enjoying a hot cup of tea and nip of rum.

This mystery runner intrigued Alf. On the race register he was listed as Mr W.H. Oami. In the coming weeks Alf would often come across him on training runs and they would plod on together, never exchanging a word. Then he would disappear whence he came.

Something else intrigued Alf. He was making a delivery for Ike at the local Art Gallery when he noticed a portrait dated 1800 of a renowned local runner, one Septimus Herne, who was known as the 'Flying Footman.' W.H. Oami was the spitting image of Herne. And another thing. The newsagent Horace Greene, blessed with an eye for such things, pointed out that 'W.H. Oami' could also read 'Who am I?' The mystery deepened.

A local historian, Professor William Bell, started digging and unearthed a story from 1810 in which Herne was said to have raced the mail coach to Market Crossford, 20 miles away. Despite having to cross five demanding hills en route Herne just pipped the coach to finish in a time of 1 hour 59 minutes.

Very few people gave Alf the run-around for long but the curious case of the mysterious W.H. Oami drove him mad before he finally uncovered the truth about the 'Flying Footman' who had been a notable runner in 1800.

Fact or fiction? The *Greystone Echo* laid down a challenge to see if any modern-day runner could repeat the feat: it would prove whether Herne's feat was indeed possible and it would be a way of flushing out W.H. Oami.

This time Oami just lost out to the coach before heading for the hills - but Alf, who finished a close third, went off in pursuit and followed the mystery runner to a secluded log cabin in the woods. There he discovered two men disguised as Septimus Herne, wearing wigs for the distinctive long hair tied in a ponytail. They turned out to be two keen club runners – one a direct descendent of the Flying Footman – who together ran a riding business that was going bankrupt. They had come up with the W.H. Oami persona – entering long races with one taking over from the other half way through – as a publicity stunt, and sure enough, now that they had been caught and their fake wins were all over the *Echo*, their business enjoyed a barrage of inquiries.

THE TOUGH OF THE TRACK

Life was tough, but Alf enjoyed nothing more on a Friday night in the winter than settling down in the warmth of Ike Smith's office to clean his spikes and dry out his running kit for the next day's cross-country race.

the kind-hearted Sam often 'forgot' to take any payment.

My word, life was tough. In the *Rover* in April 1950 we get these extraordinarily revealing descriptions of young Alf and the life he led:

His overalls had holes in them. He needed a haircut. The state of his fingernails would have caused a

manicurist to swoon. Yet, though he worked in that damp, dark welding shop that he also made his home because he did not get on with Aunt Meg, he had a great reputation as an athlete. Alf was crazy about running and jumping, and about little else – except, perhaps, eating. He was always hungry. Hard work and hard training accounted for that.

Jack of All Trades, Master of Most!

As he made his way in the world Alf's one big advantage was that he was a jack of all manual trades and a master of most. After slaving at the welding shop underneath the arches for the chronically lazy Ike Smith – who idled the day away placing bets on the horses and dogs – he moved on briefly to Greystone Aviation. But by 1951 he was working with plumber Charlie Chipping. Later that year he moved again, this time to Cougar Cars where he worked as an engineer for three months on a short-term contract. By 1952 he was employed by Brassingford Locomotives before a curious episode during which, against form, he travelled to America to study and train on a scholarship. Alf had never shown any academic inclinations thus far so we can only assume that he was virtually a professional athlete. On his return he was called into the Army on National Service – it is possible that his trademark short-back-and-sides with spiky quiff dated from this era – and he

His early morning rituals were described thus:

At half past six on the Thursday morning a bus conductor going on duty banged on the door of the welding shop as he went by. After a moment a muffled voice from inside replied, 'Thanks, mate.' Alf lay on a mattress on the floor. For pyjamas he wore his working shirt and trousers. Old coke sacks were his blankets. He yawned. As he heaved himself up he heard a rat scuttle away. He felt for his boots and put them on. He made his way round the shop to the light switch, and a small lamp burned dimly.

He crossed to the tap and filled a leaking bucket with cold water. He removed his overalls and pulled off his shirt. He had to make a search for the bit of yellow soap, and found it on the floor. He stuck his head in the bucket, pulled it out, gasping, flung water over his shoulders, and worked up a lather. He fumbled blindly for the torn roller towel.

'It'll be bread and marge for breakfast this morning,' he muttered. Alf had soon finished his meagre breakfast. He pulled off his boots and out of the drawer he took a pair of shorts, and a running vest he had bought at a second-hand shop which had the head of a timber wolf on the chest. He put on a pair of old, cracked gym shoes and tied the laces and a

nearby clock was striking seven as he opened the door; and, on this cold, misty morning, Alf padded away on a training run.

It was the only bit of time he would be able to snatch all day. Even with Ike lending a hand for once, they were only just keeping level with the work. In about half an hour Alf was back and fetching out the handcart. Through the stirring city he pushed it towards the aviation works. A wide, straight road, flanked on one side by a section of the aerodrome, led to the factory. Alf had to keep into the gutter. Buses, with their indicators at 'special', motor coaches in from distant towns, cars, motorbikes and cycles by the hundred whizzed past him. But he was out running and that was all that counted.

Alf started to apply himself more seriously to running and trying to make his way in athletics, but he was famously confrontational and more than once crossed the line from being a good-hearted working-class hero to being a pain in the backside and a social misfit. In the space of a few months he had fallen out with both the toffs at Granton Hall (where the Great Britain squad had established a state-of-the-art training camp some forty years ahead of its time) and with the perfectly sociable Greystone Harriers.

Greystone Harriers, the city club, seemed to offer him

then joined up with the Royal Artillery before ending up at the Brassingford Transport Company in 1958 which was his last known proper job, though he dabbled with sports punditry in the 1980s.

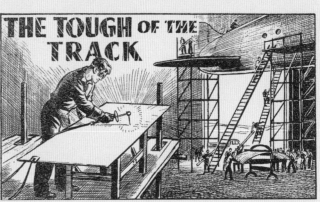

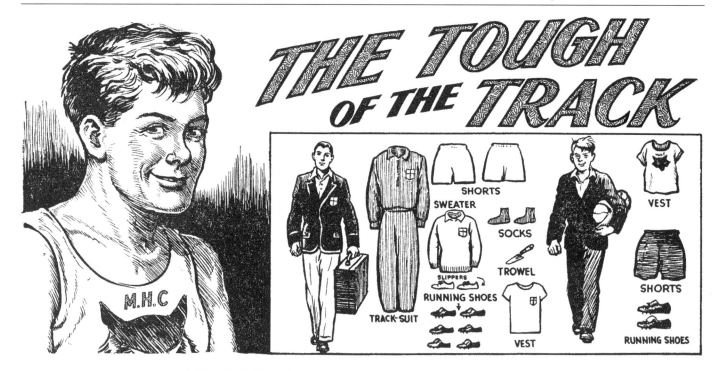

THE TOUGH OF THE TRACK

RUNNING FOR GREAT BRITAIN PRESENTED PROBLEMS

Alf was fiercely patriotic and always honoured to represent his country, but in those amateur days such calls to arms caused problems, and he often had to 'pawn' his latest prize to pay for the regulation kit required by British runners.

the best way forward, so he saved up to pay the subscription fee of half a guinea. However, he was a member for only three weeks, being instructed to return his membership card by Bob Richards, the club secretary, following a fight with Vic Mason in the 440 yards at the Greystone Harriers sports meeting.

He didn't fare much better at the Greystone Youth Club either, after a disgraceful incident in which Alf sneaked onto the athletics track early one morning to try and perfect his long-jumping technique, only to be moved on

by one Syd Castleton, the groundsman. A fracas ensued – and when Castleton stamped on his toes, Alf broke Syd's nose with a punch. That night he broke into the railway sidings to practice his jumping in the ashes there – he was nothing if not resourceful!

It was Horace Greene who, growing worried at Alf's inability to settle and get on with authority, rejuvenated his athletics career by encouraging him to enter the Layford Sports. The story is pure Tupper and would prove to be a template for the future.

BLOOMIN ADA! THOSE TOFFS AT GRANTON HALL!

The biggest motivating factor in Alf's career was putting one over the pampered Toffs at neighbouring Granton Hall, the elite training camp established for Britain's brightest young prospects, most of who appeared to be 'Varsity' types.

I AM AS GOOD AS THE NEXT MAN!

He might have been dressed in his grubby overalls, but Alf never apologised for who he was and where he came from.
Here he provides a welcome contrast to the Granton Hall crowd as a local dignitary is presented to the athletes.

The Friday night found him hitching the 75 miles from Greystone to Layford carrying his track shoes and vest in a brown paper bag – the thought of Alf owning a kitbag or rucksack at this stage of his career would clearly go against his working-class background. Only toffs could afford those, or a pair of the flash tracksuit bottoms that one or two rakish characters were beginning to wear

There was a major incident en route to race, of course; there always was. This time he cadged a lift with a lorry driver by waiting at the top of a long climb – a favourite ploy of Alf's over the years and one worth remembering if ever you find yourself on the road. All went well for a brief period, until the lorry was pulled over by a police van. Alf panicked, jumped out and started running over the fields but, much to his surprise, the 'bluebottle' who gave chase comfortably kept pace with him; and when Alf executed a double hitch-kick to clear a twenty-foot ditch, he managed to do exactly the same. Only as his uniform got muddy and heavy did he slow down enough for Alf to complete his escape. 'If every copper could run like that there would be less crime,' he thought ruefully. Then his thoughts turned to sleep, 'Oh where's a blooming haystack.'

He woke at sunrise the following morning and completed his journey by hitching a lift with the Layford milk delivery van, before seeking out a backstreet café for a fish and chips brunch and two mugs of steaming hot tea, which was to become his normal pre-race meal.

Alf arrived at the meet only to discover that he had lost a running shoe, forcing him to rush down to the local market to buy a festering old pair of spikes for a shilling – so old, in fact, that once he had them on his feet he had to tie a cord tightly around them in order to keep them together.

Alf duly beat the cursed Edgar Myers of Granton Hall – his foot was drenched in blood where the cord had cut deep. Following them home in third was an athlete called Falconer who promptly won the long jump with a classic hitch-kick and distance in excess of 22 feet. Alf gave a wolf whistle of approval and wandered over for a chat. Not a good idea! Falconer had noticed Alf had thrown his one good running spike on the brown paper bag. 'I'm the bobby who chased you last night,' he said. 'I've got the other shoe, you dropped it at the first gate we jumped.'

Falconer – who had admired Alf's runs both on the track and across the fields – reluctantly took him down to the police station and explained there had been two thousand pounds worth of stolen cigarettes in the lorry and that he would either be fined five pounds or sent to prison for a month for obstructing a police officer in his duty.

But before being charged he was asked to look at police

THE TOUGH OF THE TRACK

IT'S NOT THE CLOTHES YOU WEAR, IT'S THE MAN WHO WEARS THEM THAT COUNTS!

Alf wasn't above hamming things up a little when confronted with the Granton Hall squad. Here he decides to take his time climbing out of his grimy work overalls before tackling his pristine opponents.

photos of "men with low foreheads and sprouting ears', and was quickly able to identify his lorry driver as one Cyril Gatlow, a well-known villain. After Falconer pleaded his case, Alf escaped with a warning from Detective Superintendent Barson just in time to return to the race-track to pick up his prize.

There was, however, a problem – Mr Ramswell, the race secretary, had received reports that Alf had been heard criticizing the 30-yard allowance given to Edgar Myers in the race. A Mr Pintock was to chair a meeting to decide whether Tupper should be reprimanded and denied his rightful prize.

Meanwhile, his new friend PC Falconer had been busy making a few inquiries on Alf's behalf regarding Edgar Myers' recent performances. 'There is another man by the name of Edgar Myers,' revealed Falconer with a flourish. 'In the Bromsborough police sports, he won the mile in four minutes thirty seconds and he was second in the Castlebury Wake sports in four minutes twenty-eight. The committee must have thought it was him.

'I told you the committee has been taken for suckers,' was Alf's triumphant but rather surly reply.

Alf's athletics career progressed rapidly and soon after he'd been placed behind Rob Lackman in the Amateur Athletics Association Mile at White City, a letter arrived inviting him to run for Great Britain against France in

Paris the following week. The only problem was that before he could compete, had to buy the appropriate clothes. He gathered his life savings together and went down to Parker's the clothing shop. Alf came from an era when you had to earn everything. Unless you were lucky

YOU CAN'T ALWAYS WIN
One thing differentiating Alf and Wilson was that Alf occasionally came second and lacked the latter's aura of invincibility. Alf, however, usually avenged such defeats gloriously through hard work and guts.

THE TUPPER LEGACY LIVES ON

Many of Britain's top athletes mention Alf Tupper as their earliest inspiration and cult figure but chief among them is the former Commonwealth and European marathon champion Ron Hill, who consciously set out to emulate his hero after reading of his exploits in the *Rover* in the early 1950s.

Inspiration is what first starts people running. It can be anything from a whole host of things which sparks an individual into pulling on a pair of running shoes and experiencing that sense of independence which only running can give you. For me that inspiration came from quite an unusual hero. Although I was lucky enough to go on and participate in most of the championships he ran there was one quality which we could never share. From the very start of his career to the finish he never aged or certainly never slowed down. For my boyhood hero, who first inspired me to start running, was Alf Tupper – the Tough of the Track.

From the pages of *Rover* he set my imagination alight. Some lads read the *Wizard*, but it was my good fortune to opt for the *Rover*. Such small things can determine your life. He was immediately my man. We lived in a pretty basic two-up-two-down next to a railway with an outside loo. Alf was even worse off with his one up, one down and the awful aunt Meg. Everything seemed stacked against Alf. He lived on disused barges and under dripping railway arches. He trained at night on dimly lit paths along canal banks. Despite this – and by his own efforts – he won races. I wanted to be Alf Tupper and he inspired me to join my local club Clayton-Le-Moors Harriers. I was on my way.

No situation was too tough. No cause too hopeless. He just got on and did it. I have taken that philosophy into my life. He was just so bloody tough, it's the only word for it and I have tried to carry that mentality into my racing. I remember once I was running a 10,000 metres in Helsinki and I was up against a trio of Africans from Ethiopia. They were out to get me and three laps from the end I found myself on my back staring at the stars with a four inch scar on my ankle. Alf would have been proud of me. I just got back up and hared after them and won the race with a sprint finish down the home straight, one of my spikes just full of blood. It was pure Alf.

Other strange things happened, just like one of his stories. I was running a 10,000 metres in Trinidad once and trailing in the heat, jogging around steadily in seventh position, not gaining on anyone but nobody overtaking me either. And yet when I finished I discovered I was eighth. A runner had joined in with four or five laps to go – the officials had failed to notice apparently – and he walked off with the prize.

I have run every day of my life since 1964. For the first twenty-six years I ran twice a day, although since then I have cut it down to once a day. And the only time that record was threatened was in 1993 when I broke my sternum in a head-on crash. I had run that morning and as I was released from hospital the following day I was able to run that evening, albeit in agony and for only a mile or so. I like to think the spirit of Alf Tupper got me through that.

RUNNING – SCIENCE OR SPORT?

During one of his truces with Granton Hall the ever-willing Alf was recruited to help with a number of experiments as the 'Boffins' sought to determine the limits of human endurance.

WHO NEEDS OXYGEN?

The scientists believed that performance could be enhanced by increasing an athlete's oxygen supply, but Alf took great pleasure in disproving that theory.

WINNING BY GOING NOWHERE!

Alf astounded the scientists at Granton Hall by 'outrunning' an early version of a treadmill they had installed at their plush indoor track. They also measured him to determine his best starting position.

POETS' CORNER

ALF TUPPER

There was a man, who some say ran
For pleasure pure & sweet
Whatever type of weather
He was there pounding the streets

At the crack of dawn, he washed & yawned
Then put on his running shoes
He then set off on his training run
As the locals still did snooze

He never ran for money
As an amateur he stayed
He ran for fun to beat the best
To win was all he craved

Never ever cheated
No sarcastic quips
The secret of this mans success?
Good old fish 'n' chips

In snooty clubs where Harriers
Thought they were the best
He raced them to the finish line
Then beat them like the rest

Working class men aren't runners
We used to say at school
But Alf Tupper changed all that
As he said himself   'I run 'em all !'

As halcyon days and Alf's kind ways
Are but a distant dream
Comic heroes were our inspiration
They inspired us to succeed!

Working class men & women
That was who we knew
Who ran at Battersea Park running track
No posh athletics clubs thank you

We were Alf, not Claude or Ralph
Who had expensive spikes
A pair of shorts and plimsolls
Was what we wore on training hikes!

So cheers Alf mate!
You made us great
A role model for those
Who wanted to win so much it hurt
'I run 'em all!' our favourite prose!

By Kevin Raymond

Alf couldn't always put it in words, but he was at his happiest running free on the fells away from the grime of Greystone

HEROES

The splat of the *Rover* on lino
– Thursday's breakfast serials.
Eccentric, rebellious, lone
fighters of lost causes. Alf Tupper,
my favourite. All week I'd wonder,
had he run, plimmyless, belly full
of chips, toes in tatters, been spiked
in sight of glory by Chinless Charles
double-barrelled born to win?

Or had Alf run in hobnailed boots
after a riveting forty hours straight
thrashing metal into shape
saving the gasworks, welding
machines to life with the flame
of his oxy-acetylene torch?

My dad was an Alf lacking
the gift of Bannister legs
and lungs. But would Tupper
have coped with a wife, six kids
and every day the same cliffhanger?

By Adrian Hogan

ALWAYS TIME FOR FORTY WINKS!

So many storylines with Alf are built around him being deprived of a proper night's 'kip' before a race – having had to save somebody's life or escape from a villain. It was a common sight to see him kipping just before a race.

enough to be born a toff, the only way to better yourself was through sheer hard graft. He had to spend *£1 11s.* on some flannel trousers and *15s.* for the jacket in order to make the trip, and he paid for the extravagance by working the nightshift on the trams on top of his day job slaving for Ike.

Suited and booted to the satisfaction of the Great Britain selectors Alf was, nonetheless, the typical Brit abroad, though to be fair he was completely exhausted by all his extra shifts at work. At one point, after flying to Le Bourget airport, the distance runner Jack Sheppherd woke him up as they drove past the Eiffel Tower but he just glanced up and dismissively quipped, 'They can keep the Eiffel Tower.' Later he fell asleep at the team supper – and then again the following day he missed training after falling asleep under a tree at the Religny Stadium. It all came good, however. He was drafted into the team after Lackman turned his ankle messing around and, though Alf was still very tired and struggled for three and a half laps, once the adrenalin kicked in he won with a sprint finish. He was hailed as having run the perfect tactical race, but it was sheer fatigue that caused him to start so slowly.

For most of his career Alf shunned the limelight and confined himself to a series of seemingly nondescript local races. It was the twists and turns of the narrative, and the moral of the story, that usually counted in Alf's adventures. Occasionally, however, he broke out spectacularly.

His world record mile in 1968 was typical of the man. Alf was eating his evening meal of fish and chips from Sam Kessick's when he noticed in the local newspaper wrapped around them that the two crack American milers Don McClusky and Glen Millard, along with Sweden's Sven Huntinger, were flying back to New York from Midhampton airport the very next day, despairing of finding any decent British opposition. Alf had raced them two weeks earlier after having been forced to work through the night by Ike Smith. And on top of that, the visitors themselves had been jet-lagged. The result was a disappointingly slow race which was eventually won by McClusky.

Reading the story, Alf smelled a rat, and was not surprised the following day at the Greystone Harriers meet when it was announced over the tannoy that there were three surprise entries for the Greystone mile, which Alf had been expected to win at a canter. For once his race preparation had been perfect. A good night's sleep, no disruptive train journeys evading the police or chasing villains, no arduous night shifts mending frozen pipes or freeing passengers from train crashes. Today was his day.

They set off at a terrific pace and built steadily. Laps of fifty-nine seconds, fifty-nine and a half seconds and fifty-

FOR WHOM THE BELL TOLLS!
*Alf was famous for his devastating 'kick' on the last lap, and invariably sprang into action when the bell went,
even when exhausted and seemingly out of the race.*

eight seconds set the tone, but were only the prelude to a sensational last lap burn up – timed at fifty-three and a half seconds – between Alf, McClusky, Millard and Huntinger. Alf finished the strongest to take the race of his life by a yard in a time of three minutes fifty-one seconds exactly, ahead of the existing record which had been established by the long-striding American Jim Ryun in Bakersfield, California the previous year. In all probability this was Alf's finest pure athletic moment.

His triumph in the 1500 metres at the Helsinki Olympics in 1952 came after he had been forced to work as a chef's assistant on a ship bound for the Finnish capital. Upon docking, he jumped ship and was brought to the attention of the port officials when he outran a Finnish immigration officer down the length of the dockyard – even though his pursuer happened to be the Finland 800 and 1500 metre champion and was considered a potential medalist! Wilson, who you'll recall was in Helsinki competing in the modern pentathlon, was called to the docks to vouch for Tupper and ensure his release from custody.

Barcelona, 1992 – forty years later – was a swansong victory for the ever-popular Tupper, but of course the *real* story was how he nearly didn't compete at all, finishing fourth in the British Olympic trial behind the Grimston brothers and Joe Hawkley-Lewis, after having been 'nobbled' in the race by Hawkley-Lewis's underhand uncle. It all looked grim for Tupper until the dastardly Hawkley-Lewis injured himself, but Alf decided to make

the selectors sweat when he was called into the team – a 'will he, won't he' drama was acted out right up until the British team left for Spain. Of course nobody ever seriously believed that Alf would spurn his country and, even amidst hints of his retirement, there was never any doubt that he would triumph in Barcelona.

In 1969, the year after his world record, Alf raced against the Rakovian champion, Fedor Oranski, at White City. The race ended in a dead heat so Alf travelled to Rakovia for a rematch, adventurous stuff in the Cold War years. Unfortunately, his wallet was pinched on the way there so was forced to stowaway on board an aircraft. Upon arrival at Grovic, the Rakovian capital, he was arrested as a spy and was about to be interrogated by the secret police when he retaliated by landing a cracking left hook to the Rakovian Colonel's nose. 'Keep you hands to yourself baldy!' In a typically timely way, Alf was revealed as the famous British runner, given a compensatory plate of fish and chips – the Eastern Bloc also enjoyed a good fry-up apparently – and was rushed to the state sports stadium to run, and beat, Oranski in the 1500 metres.

Other tales were more cautionary than headline making. For a confirmed xenophobe, France featured prominently in Alf's life. Not long after his visit to Paris in 1949 he was picked as a reserve for the Great Britain team in the prestigious international cross-country meet at Aubigny, on a side packed with Granton Hall men with Commander Churcher as team manager. He was frustrated

THE TOUGH OF THE TRACK

to be the first reserve, and started bickering with Phil Rakes-Tyler who was constantly criticizing his table manners. Eventually he wandered off to a local village where he was befriended by a local welder by the name of Poppa Hartman – the only father figure who ever emerges in Alf's life – whose son, would you believe it, was a talented cross- country winner.

Alf was dramatically drafted into the team on the eve of the race, after Rakes-Tyler turned an ankle and, ignoring pleas by Churcher to run *en bloc* with the Britain team, he hatched a plan of his own, deciding to taking on the 'Flying Finn', Vuurmi, the world's best runner. It worked beautifully – Vuurmi collapsed in a heap on the fourth and final lap while Alf somehow kept going to score invaluable points by coming in twelfth and ensuring an unexpected British triumph. Churcher acknowledged the excellence of

A MEETING OF EQUALS
Alf enjoyed some of his greatest races against the 'Flying Finn' Vuurmi, at the time the world's most talented middle-distance runner. Here they clash at the prestigious Aubigny International cross-country championship in Paris in 1949.

THE TOUGH OF THE TRACK

BEWARE CROSSING WOODEN PLANK BRIDGES IN CROSS COUNTRY RACES!
There were no holds barred in the rough, tough world of Alf Tupper – Zemba the Zulu runner ensures Alf takes an early bath.

Tupper's run but Alf then blotted his copy book the following day by missing the plane home, thinking 1500 hours meant 5 p.m.! Poor Alf. It was ever thus.

On one famous occasion when he had fallen out with both Greystone Harriers and the toffs at Granton Hall, he decided to train his own team for the prestigious Clebury Road Relays, recruiting members of the Greystone Boxing Club, where he spent much of his spare time training and was a popular figure. Definitely shades of Wilson here, the master attempt-ing to impart his genius and wisdom to a novice set of runners. Except they weren't really novices. Boxers do even more road work than athletes, and Alf really believed they had an outside chance of causing a massive upset – when his good friend Clem Johnson, the local sports reporter, dropped a bombshell: Alf's team, Tupper's Trotters, were not affiliated and would be banned.

Alf was at his bolshy best in such situations. 'Nuts to that,' he raged. 'The race is run on public roads, they can't stop us. We will enter unofficially.' Which they did.

On the day, the Trotters were well behind until the fifth leg when Alf's colleague Tig ran a stormer to bring them into fifth place with Alf poised and ready to take the final leg of the race. With many points to prove, he ran like the wind and overtook Greystone Harriers, the Athletic Club de Paris and the mighty Granton Hall to win, albeit unofficially.

BAREFOOT IN THE PARK!
Running shoes always presented problems to Alf because he rarely had enough money to buy any good 'spikes'. On more than one occasion his 'runners' fell apart mid-race and he had to kick them to one side and race barefoot.

HE'S IN THE ARMY NOW

WHERE'S THERE A WILL THERE'S A WAY

A classic Alf story sees him running the final relay leg of the Inter-Regimental Sports during his National Service.
His hands had been severely burnt in a live firing accident, so he simply put the baton in his mouth!

'You can keep your blooming medals, everyone knows that my blokes were the real winners,' was Alf's predictable reply. The race generated such publicity for the boxers that they were soon receiving offers from all over the country.

One of the cameo stories that always sticks in the mind from his time in the Army was the day of the Regimental Sports when, handicapped by nasty burns to his hands after an unfortunate accident during a tear-gas drill, he bravely competed and claimed a second place in the 200 metres for his regiment before winning the 1500 metres. By the time it came to the 4 x 400 metre relay, which they had to win to take the divisional trophy, all appeared lost. But an inspired piece of improvisation from Alf, who ran the last leg with the baton in his mouth to save his blistered hands, saw his team home to victory.

In 1986 Alf saw an article in a local newspaper – as ever he was eating his fish and chips at the time – claiming that on 1 April 1920 a local chap by the name of

Samuel Granger had run around Hillstone Lake, a distance of 5123 metres (3.1 miles) in thirteen minutes and thirty-eight seconds, a race apparently notable for the appearance of 'a monster' in the lake during the run. Granger had set up a prize fund to be donated to a charity chosen by any runner capable of equalling or even bettering his time.

Ken Waters, an instructor at the Ashdale Youth Centre, was trying to train his runners to win the prize – they desperately needed an injection of cash to carry out repairs to their building. Alf was more than delighted to give it a go on behalf of the youth centre, but despite training every day with a relay squad of lads from the club he always came home some thirty seconds adrift.

On the day of the challenge, Alf went flat out, but was still running outside of the time he needed – until, from out of the water, a shape appeared … the monster! Alf immediately lost all signs of tiredness and sprinted for the tape, breaking the record by a full five seconds! The monster had been nothing more than a stunt pulled on Alf by the

LITTER LOUTS WILL BE FINED
One of the strangest-ever Alf stories saw him become a born-again litter policeman, waging war on anybody who soiled the streets — he even stopped mid-race at the White City to retrieve rubbish blowing across the track.

young runners to help him home. When he finally twigged that Samuel had set the record on *April Fool's Day*, 1920, he had to chuckle. April fool or no fool, he still collected the money the youth centre so badly needed.

Perhaps the most intriguing tale concerning Alf was his brief and unlikely stint as a litter policeman. Alf was celebrating a good night's training with a portion of Sam Kessick's best fish and chips. In true Alf fashion, he scoffed the lot and threw the paper on the pavement, only to be accosted for littering by 'Battling Betty', a local no-nonsense WPC. As a result of Betty's lecture, which was fur-

ther driven home when he trod on a piece of carelessly discarded broken glass which hampered his training, Alf become a convert; a zealot, in fact, in the war against litter.

On his next race day, Alf was winning easily but suddenly became distracted by a flying piece of litter. He amazed the crowd by grabbing the rubbish, leaving the race in search of a bin to put it in, and then returning to the track in time to win the race! The urban street fighter could also, it seemed, set a good example.

ALLEZ, ALLEZ
Trouble followed Alf wherever he went. A seemingly innocent invitation to run for a small French village against their neighbours on his way back from Paris ended in full-scale riots as ancient grudges were fought out.

Alf Shrubb – The Model for Alf Tupper?

The myth and cult status afforded to Alf Tupper has undoubtedly been enhanced by some confusion in the minds of sports fans between him and another 'great' of British distance running, Alf Shrubb. At the turn of the twentieth century Shrubb was the world's greatest runner but attempts were made to airbrush him from athletics history after he committed the cardinal sin – in the eyes of the athletics establishment – of becoming professional and running for money.

Alf Shrubb was was born and lived just outside Horsham and was the lowly son of a farmhand. He trained as a brickie and a carpenter before discovering his genius for running, in true Tough of the Track fashion, by racing a horse-driven fire tender for three miles to a burning cottage in nearby Southwater – and winning! The fire officer was a member of the local running club and immediately suggested he joined

There was a tragicomic quality to Shrubb which mirrored what we see in Tupper – a working-class hero who was always kicking against the Establishment and the toffs. Later in his career Shrubb staged a series of races against a mysterious American Indian called Tom Longboat, and earned a living by entering, and winning, numerous man versus horse contests in North America.

Less than nine stone when dripping wet, he was dubbed the 'Little Wonder' early in his career and used to train two or three times a day, a revolutionary regime in those days. He was also convinced of the qualities of King & Barnes Old Ale, which he used to sup most nights – walking three miles to his local pub and briskly walking the three miles back. Alf Tupper had his fish and chips, Alf Shrubb had his ale.

Guy Fawkes' Night 1904 was when Shrubb exploded into the limelight with the run of his life at Ibrox Park in Glasgow, home of Rangers. Accompanied throughout, at his request, by a massed band of pipers who played stirring music in the centre of the arena, Shrubb broke world records, amateur and professional, at every distance from 5 to 10 miles in one single run. After accepting the crowds' congratulations, he went on to establish a world one-hour record of 11 miles 1137 yards. It would be forty-nine years before a British runner, Gordon Pirie, broke another world distance record of any description. And in the same year, 1953, the Scotsman Ian Binnie finally improved Shrubb's hour record by 200 yards.

His 10 mile world record, the most prestigious distance at the time, of fifty minutes 40.6 seconds lasted twenty-four years until it was finally beaten in 1928 by

Alf Shrubb was a real-life multi-world-record-holder and local boy made good from Sussex. He and Alf Tupper were often mistaken for one another in the public's mind – adding to the reputation of both!

the 'Flying Finn' Paavo Nurmi, and remained a British record until 1936 when it was improved by William Eaton. In the same year, Eaton finally broke through Shrubb's six-mile time of twenty-nine minutes 59.4 seconds.

Brendan Foster sums it up well:

Shrubb's times are still impressive by today's standards, but are nothing short of sensational given that they were set 100 years ago on a dodgy track virtually in the middle of winter. I first heard his name back in 1978 when I crowned my best year by breaking the world 10,000 metres record. Stan Greenberg, the statistician, came up afterwards and said I was the first man to hold British records at 1500-, 3000-, 5000 and 10,000 metres – or the equivalent – since Alf Shrubb in 1904. 'Alf who?' was my response, but ever since then I've loved reading little snippets about his life and career.

He was definitely an Alf Tupper character, the original template – Tupper was my hero as a schoolboy. Shrubb was a pioneer and had to be a bit of a showman to earn recognition, but there can be no doubting his extraordinary talent. He deserves a place of honour in the roll call of British athletics.

THE TOUGH OF THE TRACK

THE BLIZZARD AT BRIDGELY.

SNOW had been drifting down lightly at the start of the Three Counties cross-country race at Bridgely, but soon after the runners had completed a couple of laps, the wind rose, the snow thickened, and Alf Tupper, the Tough of the Track, lost sight of Harden-Hughes, who was leading the field.

Alf plodded on. The wind howled and a line of spruce trees bent over in the gusts. It was impossible to see for more than a few yards.

"Lummy," muttered Alf grimly, "this is a nice afternoon out !"

He reached a ditch and only after a search found the plank that spanned the icy water. Through the driving snow he located a Dutch barn that showed him he was still on his course.

Alf shivered and ran past the barn. Running was his sport. In the summer months he had had a successful season on the track. He couldn't bear the idea of laying off during the winter, so he had taken up cross-country running. He lived in Greystone, a large manufacturing town, and as plumber's mate to Charlie Chipping.

The Tough made out a windmill that gave him his bearings. He battled his way over the summit and found the going a bit easier down the slope. But it required a search to find the way into the sunken lane that led back towards Bridgely village, the finishing point.

Already the snow was forming drifts and Alf ran into a patch in which he sunk up to his knees. He forged through and trudged on. He was plastered with snow. It lay thick in his shaggy hair.

Through another drift he emerged from the lane. Now he was facing north-east and full into the wind. He had to keep his head right down to breathe. An oak tree gave him his bearings and then, out of the blizzard, came the shape of Bridgely School from which the race had started and which was also the finishing point.

Alf plodded slowly towards the building. He peered round and scowled angrily.

"Why aren't the blooming judges on the job ?" he growled, for nobody was to be seen.

Alf turned in through the school gateway. Lights were shining from the windows, for the building was being used as a dressing-room.

There were shouts of "shut that door" as he pushed it open and stood on the threshold.

His blurred eyes picked out Harden-Hughes, the famous cross-country runner.

"So you beat me to it, Noel !" he exclaimed.

Harden-Hughes stared at him in amazement.

"You haven't finished the course ?" he gasped.

Alf stared at him in surprise. "What d'you suppose I've been doing—looking for birds' nests ?" he scoffed.

Stewart Farr, the secretary of the Three Counties Association, came forward.

"The race was abandoned," he said. "It wasn't fit for a dog to be out—and we abandoned it after the second lap."

"I was out in it," snapped Alf. He gave a sniff as he looked down the room at the other competitors, most of whom had finished changing. "Lot of cissies !"

"I admire your pluck, Tupper," declared Farr, "but I'm afraid that as the race was abandoned, we can't award you a medal."

Alf raised a grin.

"Don't make me cry," he said. "I'd sooner have a cuppa tea than a box of medals."

"We can give you a cup of tea," replied Farr.

Alf thawed out a bit by the stove and got out of his sodden running togs. He dressed in shirt, trousers, sports jacket, and boots. He never wore under-vest, pull-over, or socks. Round his neck he tied a muffler and then he put on his prized rain-coat that he only wore on rare occasions. He wrapped up his running things and shoes in a piece of brown paper and was ready to go.

It took the bus two hours to cover a distance that ordinarily would have required half an hour.

Alf's feet were cold but he did not keep sniffing and sneezing, like many of the other athletes in the vehicle.

Harden-Hughes, muffled up in a thick overcoat, sat next to Alf.

"What are you shaking for, Noel ?" the Tough asked.

"I'm frozen to the marrow," replied Harden-Hughes, his teeth chattering. "I'll get in a hot bath as soon as I get home and then go to bed."

When the bus put down its passengers at Greystone, Alf made for the small cafe kept by Sam Kessick near the railway viaduct.

The cafe was suffocatingly hot but Alf sniffed appreciatively at the aroma of boiling fat and fried fish and chips.

"Six penn'orth of chips and a piece, Sam," he said.

Kessick stared at him from his one bright eye.

"You ain't been running this afternoon ?" he exclaimed.

"I'm about the only one who did," grunted Alf. "I can't make some chaps out. Just because it started to snow a bit they packed up."

Alf enjoyed his fish and chips and swilled them down with a couple of cups of tea.

"That's better," he said to Kessick. "I'll be off home now."

Snow plastered him again by the time he reached the disused canal basin in which lay a derelict canal boat. He sprang aboard and hauled open the creaking door of the cabin, roofed now with a sheet of corrugated iron.

He lit a candle and pulled open the damper of the stove. He never lacked for fuel. There was plenty of coal to be excavated from the mud, as coal barges had at one time been unloaded at the wharf.

Alf sat on the edge of the bunk to take off his boots.

"It ain't been a bad day out," he muttered. "Just the same, there ain't the thrill in cross-country running that you get on the track—not for me, anyway."

PIPES TO MEND.

SNOW lay thickly around but the sky was clear and frosty when Alf pushed open the door of Charlie Chipping's shop on Monday morning. The room was crammed with such objects as cisterns and galvanised iron tanks.

With his bowler hat on the back of his head, Chipping was taking a message on the phone. He had the kind of moustache usually seen on the face of a walrus and, because of the cold, a ripe, red nose.

He hung up the phone and greeted Alf with a nod.

"That's the tenth," he said.

"The tenth what ?" asked Alf.

"The tenth burst pipe to be reported this morning," stated the plumber.

Alf started to collect the tools and Chipping filled the containers of their blow-lamps.

"So your race was abandoned on Saturday," he remarked.

"Ay," grunted Alf. "It was a blooming frost !"

Chipping, who had done some running in his younger days, put down the petrol can.

"Is this cross-country racing doing you any good, Alf ?" he demanded. "You're a track man. You had a champion season during the summer. Ain't you backing the wrong hoss in tackling these cross-country races ?"

"I'd be bored stiff without a bit of racing, Charlie," replied Alf.

"That ain't the point," retorted the plumber. "That's a short-sighted way of looking at things. When I was a young 'un, our trainer was Tom Woods. You wouldn't know of him now, but he was right on top of his job—did it as a hobby, of course. Well, Tom always used to tell us that runs, but not races, across country were to be recommended for keeping fit. He was dead against a track man racing in the winter."

Alf listened intently.

"He was up against racing, was he ?" he muttered.

"Right up against it," said Chipping. "Have a run in the country, yes, he used to tell us. Race across country, no, he'd say."

The phone rang and Chipping answered the call. He hung up the receiver.

"The lady at fifteen Belmont Street, has got a blooming fountain playing in her back kitchen and don't know where to turn off the water," he reported. "We'll call there first, Alf."

With Alf shoving the hand-cart and Chipping resting a hand on the side, they left the shop and started out on their day of mending burst pipes.

They had reached the High Street when Alf let go the handle and let the hand-cart come to a stop.

There was curiosity in his eyes as he stared across at three young men, hatless, but muffled up in scarves and overcoats, who were walking along the opposite pavement.

"Lummy, I thought Cal Marrow had gone back home," he exclaimed.

"Which one is Cal Marrow?" asked Chipping.

Alf pointed to the bronzed young man in the middle of the three. Marrow was the American runner who had had great success on British tracks during the season. The Tough had beaten him once, but that had been Marrow's only defeat.

The tallest of the group paused to look in a shop window and Alf could see his keen features with a long, prominent nose and a chin which stuck out like the point of a new moon.

"I've placed him, too," gasped Alf. "I've seen pictures and cartoons of him in the papers and if he isn't Frank Ferris, I'll shove this cart up a lamp-post."

"Ferris?" echoed Chipping. "The chap who won all them track events in the Empire Games in New Zealand?"

"That's him or I'm a corkscrew," said Alf. "He didn't half set up some cracking times. I was hoping he'd be over for the summer, but he had to stay in Australia to pass an exam or something."

Chipping shifted his gaze to the third and burliest of the group, a young fellow with a broad chest, a swarthy complexion and sleek dark hair brushed straight back.

"Know him?" he asked.

Alf's excitement grew.

"I've placed him," he burst out. "I saw him running in the sprints when I was over at Brussels for the European Games. Yes, he's Peter Vurmi—the chap from Finland."

A pompous policeman came over.

"You can't park that hand-cart here," he snapped.

"Okay, Cecil, we're just off," said Alf and got hold of the handle again.

But he had pushed the truck only a few yards when he pulled up with a jerk at the sight of another athletic young man who had come out of a shop and joined the others.

"Well, chase me, that's Ken Bakerson," he gulped.

"The high jumper," said Chipping.

"That's him!" exclaimed Alf. "He can clear six feet six any time he feels like it. I'd like to know what all these chaps are doing here at this time of the year?"

"Maybe they're having a do at Granton Hall," suggested the plumber.

"Charlie, I guess you're right," Alf said.

Granton Hall, a large house on the outskirts of Greystone, had been turned into an athletics coaching centre.

"Maybe they're having some kind of winter coaching stunt with lectures or something," added Alf. "They can keep their lectures. They're too blooming highbrow for me."

⊞▲▲▲▲▲▲▲▲▲▲▲▲▲▲▲⊞
ALF AFLOAT.
⊞▼▼▼▼▼▼▼▼▼▼▼▼▼▼▼⊞

WITH thaw and frost alternating, Alf and Chipping spent some busy days.

In mid-week the thaw won. The snow melted so fast that streets were awash and then came a deluge of rain.

On Wednesday evening, as he stood in his doorway and looked at the rain, Chipping remarked, "You won't!"

"What?" asked Alf.

"Run at Kempley on Saturday," said the plumber. "The fields are low-lying. They'll be flooded."

"It'll be a wasted week-end if I don't have a race," replied Alf dolefully.

"Then you're not minding what I told you?" exclaimed the plumber.

"Oh, I guess maybe I'll cut the cross-country races out later," Alf said, but he had an uncomfortable feeling that Chipping was right and that these ten miles cross-country races and the training for them, were not suitable for a track man.

Alf was sopping wet when he got to his canal boat home.

He let his clothes dry on him in front of the stove and fried himself some sausages for his supper.

As he had no wireless to listen to, or anything to read, he turned early into the bunk, sleeping in his shirt under a couple of blankets.

Daylight was filtering in when he woke up, stretched and yawned. Then he jerked up on his elbow. He could hear the lapping of water, he could hear creaks. He felt that the old craft was moving.

Alf thrust his legs out of the bunk and uttered a yell of surprise when he found he was nearly knee-deep in water.

He waded to the door and hauled it open.

"Lummy," he gasped. "I'm off for a cruise."

It was no doubt the rapid thaw and the deluge that had filled the basin and lifted the boat off the mud in which it had rested for so long. While Alf had been asleep it had drifted to the middle of the basin, twenty or thirty yards away from the wharf.

Alf scrambled out. He looked towards the bow and saw it was under water.

"I'm sinking," he muttered. "The old hooker's sinking—and I'll go with it unless somebody comes along pretty sharp."

But warehouses backed on the wharf and the only moving thing was a dog.

Alf plunged back into the cabin. His idea was to salvage his belongings. He rammed his clothes, after putting on his trousers and overalls, into his fibre suitcase and lifted it on to the roof of the cabin. He fetched out the biscuit barrel, won as a prize for running, in which he kept his bit of margarine and lard, and the mug he used for his tea. The only other trophy of the track he could get at was a cruet.

Alf climbed up on to the roof and crouched there while the canal boat sank lower and lower. There was a small boat tied up to the wharf but nobody in sight to man it and row to his rescue. He hollered but there was no reply.

The Tough could swim, but not well. But it looked as if he were not going to get any option. In case the necessity came, he knotted his bootlaces together, tying the biscuit barrel and the cruet to them, and hung his boots round his neck.

Alf could hear the distant roar of traffic, but for all the help he got, he might have been sinking in the middle of the Pacific.

The boat sank till water started to creep across the roof of the cabin.

Alf took a deep breath and slid into the freezing water. Pushing the suitcase ahead of him he struck out clumsily for the wharf.

It was his toughness that enabled him to resist the cold and to keep going, but by the time he reached the steps and climbed out, he could not have stood much more.

His limbs were blue with cold and his teeth were chattering. The wind howled round him as, with water dripping from his soaked clothes, he hurried to the plumber's.

The first thing he saw was a note for him on the mantelpiece. Chipping had written—"Follow me along to Granton Hall with the hand-cart. I've had to go off without you as the Warden wants to see me."

"You'll have to wait a bit, Charlie," muttered Alf as, with shaking hands, he struck a match and lit the gas fire. "I'm going to dry out a bit, and have a cuppa tea and a bite, before I start work."

When, in due course, Alf pushed the hand-cart up the drive of Granton Hall, Chipping came to meet him.

"What's been keeping you, Alf?" he asked.

"My Home Sweet Home got sunk this morning," said Alf, and described what had happened.

"That was a bit of bad luck," exclaimed the plumber. "You'll have to go into lodgings."

"Not if I can blooming well help it," declared the Tough. "I don't get on with landladies. But what's the job up here, Charlie?"

"There are lots of jobs to do," Chipping answered. "They all come about through the big building at the back of the house, that used to be the gymnasium, being turned into an indoor sports arena with track and everything."

Alf blinked.

"An indoor arena with track!" he gasped.

"We're going round there now," stated the plumber. "Our job is down in the cellars, but there's nobody to stop you having a look-see."

Alf took the hand-cart along at a gallop. At the rear of the house loomed the large structure that had been built originally as a private theatre and subsequently turned into a gymnasium. Now, apparently, it was undergoing another conversion.

The doors were open and Alf walked in.

He slithered to a stop and his eyes opened wide at the sight of the running-track, banked on the curves, that had been constructed round the interior of the building. It had a composition surface such as was used on the best outdoor tracks but, inside it, was a smaller wooden track. At one side of the building was a balcony backed by a number of glass-fronted cubicles.

A huge clock had an unusual face—with three hands, one for minutes, one for seconds, and the third for recording tenths of a second. Metal standards that were topped by what looked like box-aerials stood at regular intervals round the track. Within the oval there was a jumping pit with other equipment of which Alf could not get the hang at all.

"Lummy, Charlie, it looks as if the lucky blighters are going to get in some winter track practice here," exclaimed Alf, his eyes gleaming.

"Maybe this explains it," said the plumber.

"Explains what?" asked Alf.

"Why Cal Marrow, Frank Ferris, and the other top-notchers are in the town," said Chipping. "They're here to keep themselves in trim during the winter."

"Ay, that would be it," replied Alf. "Gee, but don't that track look a dream! D'you say we're coming up here quite a lot?"

"Yes, and that reminds me we ought to be down in the cellar connecting up the heating apparatus," Chipping said.

"Okay, I'll come along," said Alf. "But I'm having a run round that track before I'm much older."

"I don't see that there'll be anyone to stop you so long as you pick your time," replied Chipping.

⊞▲▲▲▲▲▲▲▲▲▲▲▲▲▲▲⊞
THE GRANTON HALL TRACK.
⊞▼▼▼▼▼▼▼▼▼▼▼▼▼▼▼⊞

ALF and Chipping had not guessed right when they thought the indoor arena was merely for winter training.

That afternoon quite a number of newspaper reporters visited Granton Hall by invitation, and assembled in the main hall of the house.

The Warden of the Centre, Commander Harold Churcher,

who was a former Olympics relay runner, came in. He was accompanied by a middle-aged man with a shock of unruly grey hair and a thin, precise-looking individual who wore rimless glasses. Then several athletes, wearing the ties and badges of some of the most famous clubs in the world, entered and formed a group at the side.

There were whispers among the reporters. They had recognised the man as Professor Hugo Dane and Professor Lee-Latham, two eminent scientists.

Commander Churcher was the spokesman.

" We have brought you here to give an outline of important, not to say vital, experiments that are to be carried out at Granton Hall during the coming months," he stated. " These experiments will form the first real scientific inquiry into athletics, and we hope at the end to be able to answer many questions that are baffling us at the moment. We shall be concerned with tests of human endurance, of human speed, with problems of stamina, of diet, and breathing, to mention but a few."

He paused for a moment while the reporters made notes.

" We hope to learn a great deal," he then went on. " More than that, our experiments may well lead to greater athletic performances in the future. We have constructed an indoor sports arena in which we shall be able to make our tests under perfect conditions and with the help of the most-up-to-date apparatus. It will, for instance, be possible to measure and record the speed of a runner at any point in a race. It will be equally possible to record the exhaustion he is feeling. It will be possible to establish the rate of movement that best suits a man. We also anticipate some extraordinary results from artificial pacing."

" You're making a real science of running, then ?" exclaimed a sporting journalist.

" Yes, this will be a laboratory for athletics," chuckled Commander Churcher. " Professor Hugo Dane and Professor Lee-Latham will be resident here for most of the time, and we shall have the help of some of the outstanding athletes of Europe and America to serve as subjects in the experiments. From time to time we shall issue statements of what we are doing, and some, at least, of the events will be seen by you newspaper reporters."

After more questions had been asked and answered, there was a move to the indoor arena.

Professor Lee-Latham took some of the reporters into one of the glass-fronted cubicles to show them the recording instruments.

" Frank Figgis is going to run a lap of the track—two hundred and twenty yards—for us," he said. " His progress will be measured by a series of photo-electric cells placed at ten yard intervals round the track. You will be able to watch his speed on this dial, which looks rather like a car speedometer. At the same time his run will be recorded on this other instrument—the speedo-

graph—by a pen drawing a line on a piece of graph paper fixed on to a revolving cylinder."

The newspaper men watched with interest. Down below, Figgis was stripping off his track suit.

Commander Churcher, who had stayed below, pressed down the master switch. A red light glowed above the clock to indicate that all the apparatus was alive.

Nobody noticed faces peering out of the half-open doorway that led down to the cellar. Alf and Charlie Chipping were having a look.

Frank Hamilton, the track coach, took up his position by a stand to which the starting-pistol was fixed. A reporter was curious about this.

" Why doesn't he hold the pistol ?" he inquired.

" There is an electrical lead from the pistol so that we can record the precise instant at which it is fired and so ascertain how fast

Readers Who Sent in Their School Badges

There has been a great response to the request for school badges. The first lot sent in by readers appears on this week's front cover. They came from the following boys:—

John Marshall, 19 Daneswell Drive, Wirral, Cheshire.
W. A. Gunn of Nottingham.
J. J. Maxwell, 68 Tysoe Ave., Enfield, Middlesex.
G. Ritchie, 16 Larchfield Ave., Newton Mearns.
J. C. Hayes, 6 Well Close Mt., Leeds, 7. ·
J. M'Ellin, 1 The Ridge, Shirehampton, Bristol.
M. W. Jones, 50 Wolseley Rd., St. Helens.
J. A. Knowles, 15 Talbot St., St Helens.
Donald Stewart, 40 Colinslee Ave., Paisley.
E. R. Biggadike, 26 Shakespeare Rd., Kettering.
Gwyn Thomas, 2 Eileen Pl., Treherbert, Glam.
A. C. Allen, Folkeswood Cottages, Hythe, Kent.
D. N. Vickers, Ashville College, Harrogate.
A. J. Bennett of Newport.
D. Bourne, 68 Dimsdale Rd., Birmingham.
T. Dolly of Heaton, Bradford.
C. S. Smith of Uxbridge.
B. Kybett, 49 Market St., Llanelly.
P. Astles, 57 Delamere St., Winsford, Cheshire.

Other school badges will appear in future issues of " The Rover." Look out for them ! What about your school? Has it got a badge? Let's hear about it.

the runner responds," explained Lee-Latham.

Hamilton used the customary words of command.

" Get to your mark. Get set !"

At the crack of the pistol it seemed as if Figgis hit his stride instantly, but Lee-Latham pointed out there was a lag of half a second before he was really on the move.

As Figgis sped round the track, the needle on the recording dial flickered and the pen traced his course on the graph paper.

" Ah, he has done the distance in the good time of twenty-one and nine-tenths seconds," exclaimed Lee-Latham. " You will notice from the recording that he attained his maximum speed between the sixty and eighty yards posts, where his speed was eleven and a half yards per second."

On the cellar steps, Chipping gave Alf a tap on the shoulder.

" We'd better get on with our work," he said.

Alf gave a nod.

" Ay, the fun seems to be over," he replied. " But the next time we come along here I'll bring my running-strip."

" That'll be to-morrow," said

the plumber. " By the way, Alf, where are you going to hang out now your boat is sunk ? There isn't room round at my house."

" Aw, I'll doss down at the shop till I find a place," answered Alf.

ALF TRIES THE TRACK.

ON the following morning Cal Marrow strode round the track. He was running the mile and the scientists watched his progress on the instruments.

As he completed the eight laps and flashed over the timing strip, the clock recorded four minutes ten seconds.

Lee-Latham pointed to the graph.

" It is a splendid piece of running !" he exclaimed. " You will note that the first quarter-mile was a shade the fastest, that he then had two even quarters and, thanks to his finishing spurt, clipped a tenth of a second off the final lap. It was

a rhythmic, even effort——"

" The only way to run a race is evenly," said Hugo Dane in his gruff voice. " The runner who goes in fits and starts will never set up a good time."

The indoor arena emptied as the scientists and runners went away to their lunch.

Hardly had the outer door closed than up popped Alf from the cellar followed by Chipping. He took off his plumber's clothing and threw it over a barrier. He was wearing his running kit underneath.

" What are you going to have a go at ?" asked Chipping.

" The mile, pal," said Alf.

" Here ! Let me start the clock. I watched how he done it," exclaimed Chipping.

" Okay," replied Alf.

Chipping pulled down the master switch. A few moments later the Tough sped away over the starting strip.

After the rough, wet, sticky going of cross-country running, it felt grand to have a fast, springy track under his feet again.

Chipping watched Alf and he kept an eye on the clock.

" Buck your ideas up, Alf,"

he shouted after the Tough ha run a quarter of a mile.

Alf was warm now. He ha been working in the cold cella all morning and he had starte rather chilly and cramped. H went hard for the next 440 yard

On going into the next lap h felt a twinge in the calf of hi right leg. It slowed him righ down. It was just a touch o cramp and it went as suddenl as it came.

With a quarter of a mile to go the Tough glanced up at th clock.

" Lummy, have I been stand ing still ?" he thought and whipped himself into a tre mendous burst of speed.

Chipping shook his head.

" He won't keep this up," h growled, but Alf did and th clock was on four minutes seven and a half seconds as he finishec with a spurt that took al his wind and left him tucked uj and panting.

Chipping shut the maste switch and the clock hand returned to zero.

In the middle of the afternoor Commander Churcher and th two scientists returned to th indoor arena to prepare for som more running. They climbec the steps to the balcony anc entered the cubicle.

" I was very impressed b the even nature of Marrow's running," remarked Dane. " H showed a fine sense of the pac judgment essential for running a fast mile and——"

An astonished cry broke from Lee-Latham.

" Look at this !" he exclaimed and peered at the speedograph " What's happened ? It ha recorded a mile in under fou minutes eight seconds."

" It looks more like the recorc of an earthquake," gasped Dane as he studied the erratic line.

The quarter-mile timings a which they stared indicated a sluggish first quarter, a lightning second, a slow third, and a jet propelled final.

" It's all wrong," declarec Lee-Latham. " Nobody coulc run such a mile."

" No, no, it's impossible," agreed Dane. " The apparatus must have been left on and something shook the instrument and caused it to revolve."

" Yes, that's what happened," said Lee-Latham. " All our athletes were at lunch. Nobody has been having a private trial. We had better check up on the instruments before we start the afternoon's programme——"

Dane turned his head in a listening attitude.

" D'you hear hammering, Churcher ?" he asked. " Can you hear a clanking sound ?"

Churcher nodded lightly.

" The plumbers are working in the cellar," he said. " That's all it is."

" That may explain it," said Lee-Latham. " Their knockings may have started off the speedo-graph."

" Quite likely," agreed Dane. He gave a gruff laugh. " We'll blame it on the plumber."

Next week Alf gives the professors another shock — in a record-smashing 220 yards!

MELCHESTER ROVERS F.C.
WINNERS OF THE EUROPEAN CUP-WINNERS' CUP

Standing, L. to R.:

"TAFFY" MORGAN (TRAINER)   DEREK COOPER   "JUMBO" TRUDGEON   KEN MILLAR   "TUBBY" MORTON   TONY STORME   TOM DAWSON   BEN GALLOWAY (MANAGER)

Seated, L. to R.:

"BOMBER" REEVES   "BUSTER" BROWN   ROY RACE (CAPTAIN)   "BLACKIE" GRAY   "OSSIE" JONES

ROY'S HONOURS
WHEN PLAYING OR MANAGING MELCHESTER ROVERS

1957-58 League Champions	**1974-75** European Cup Winners' Cup winners
1958-59 FA Cup winners	**1976-77** League Champions
1959-60 League Champions	**1977-78** Beaten in European Cup final
1960-61 FA Cup winners	**1978-79** UEFA Cup winners
1962-63 League Champions	**1979-80** League Champions
1963-64 European Cup winners	**1981-82** Second Division Champions
1964-65 World Club Cup winners	**1983-84** FA Cup winners
1965-66 FA Cup winners	**1984-85** European Cup Winners' Cup winners
1966-67 European Cup Winners' Cup winners	**1985-86** Milk Cup winners
1967-68 League Champions	**1986-87** Littlewoods Cup winners
1968-69 European Cup winners	**1987-88** League Champions
1969-70 World Club Cup winners	**1989-90** FA Cup winners
FA Cup winners	**1991-92** League Champions
1970-71 European Cup Winners' Cup winners	**1998-99** FA Cup winners
1971-72 League Champions	
FA Cup winners	
1972-73 European Cup winners	
1973-74 League Cup winners	
FA Cup winners	

Summary:

World Club Cup (2); European Cup (3); European Cup Winners' Cup (8); UEFA Cup (1) FA Cup (9) League Cup/Littlewoods/Milk Cup (3).

ROY OF THE ROVERS
An English Institution

Roy Race – Roy of the Rovers to most of the football-playing world – was the greatest and certainly most successful footballer this country has ever known, a superhero to rank up there with the best of them. Physically and temperamentally he appeared to be the ultimate hybrid, a man who possessed the strength and power of the late great Duncan Edwards, the poise and anticipation of England World Cup hero Bobby Moore and the predatory striking instincts of a modern-day Alan Shearer. Roll them all into one and you have a considerable player, not to mention a notable human being.

Unlike Wilson of the *Wizard* and Alf 'Tough of the Track' Tupper, there is – at least on the surface of it – little air of mystery, astonishment or controversy to Roy. From the moment he arrived on the scene in 1955, it appeared that he was a fully-fledged world champion. His stories draw their suspense from hearing about the various methods that his opponents employed to defuse that astonishing talent. His story of endless success and fame could well have become a little bland, but Roy endured more than his fair share of dramas and tragedy as well; he was no stranger to suffering, and understood that just as the gods give, they also take away.

He is the only one of our heroes who enjoyed a love life and marriage, albeit that it was the gorgeous Penny who had to pop the question and not vice versa. Their married life was certainly eventful. They had three children – Roy Junior, Melinda and Diana – but separated for a while when Roy went through a crisis of confidence seven years into the marriage; and then he shocked friends and foe alike by leaving his beloved team, Melchester, for a short while. He nearly died following a now infamous attempted shooting in 1981, but Penny nursed him throughout the ordeal with

all the devotion of a Florence Nightingale until he emerged once again, perhaps a stronger man. Later still he was in very low spirits when his left foot – his strongest on the pitch – had to be amputated following a helicopter crash in Italy. And then came the final blow: Penny's mysterious death in an unexplained car crash.

No, life with Roy was never bland or boring. He went through it all, the gamut of highs and lows, taking us with him as we followed and supported from the sidelines. His work ethic was tremendous and there often appears to be an implicitly moral element to his stories of overcoming all the odds and misfortunes through a very English attitude of persistence and courage. 'Don't just play like me, behave like me' is the lesson we learned from Roy.

But enough of this, let's not indulge in the post-match inquest before the action has begun to unfold. Let's relive some of Roy's finest, and most painful, moments.

EARLY DAYS

Roy was an only child and, as the grandson of the former Melchester Rovers captain Billy Race, he was almost destined for a life in football. His family lived on a modest housing estate in Melchester and the value of hard work and honesty was drummed into him at an early stage. In the post-war years, austerity was evident everywhere for Roy, as it was for Alf Tupper, although to a lesser degree. The climb to the top was hard earned and had to be well merited. There was a certain nobility in that. Initially he appears to have failed the eleven-plus but through sheer application Roy showed himself to be

ROY RACE HAD RECENTLY STARTED AT HIS NEW SCHOOL IN MELCHESTER, AND HIS FOOTBALLING ABILITY SOON GAINED HIM A PLACE IN THE SCHOOL'S UNDER-15 TEAM. BUT IN HIS FIRST MATCH, BECAUSE OF THE SCHEMING OF HIS RIVAL BERT BESTON, ROY—WITH HIS PAL BLACKIE GRAY—ARRIVED LATE AND MISSED THE KICK-OFF. MELCHESTER WERE DISHEARTENED AND WERE LOSING 3-0. ROY MANAGED TO SCORE ONE GOAL . . .

AT HALF-TIME THE CAPTAIN GAVE THE PLAYERS HIS PLAN FOR THE SECOND HALF...

ROY'S THE ONE WHO CAN SCORE—SO KEEP PUSHING THE BALL TO HIM ALL THE TIME.

...AND ROY KEEPS BANGING THE BALL PAST THEIR GOALKEEPER!

IT'S A TALL ORDER—BUT I'LL DO MY BEST.

TEAM-MATES LOOKED TO ROY, EVEN AT SCHOOL

Melchester GS found themselves 3-0 down at half-time after Roy and Blackie Gray had been sent on a wild goose chase by the scheming Bert Beston. But all was not lost. No game was beyond retrieval when you had Roy in your side.

THERE WAS NEVER ANY DOUBT ROY WOULD BECOME A PROFESSIONAL FOOTBALLER

From the first moment Roy walked into Melchester Stadium as a schoolboy he knew exactly what he wanted to do in life.
It was an inspiring moment and one he remembered fondly.

a model schoolboy, and in 1951, at the age of fourteen, he was transferred across to the prestigious Melchester Grammar School. The characteristics that marked his glittering career shone through at an early age – Roy was courageous, fearless, upright, modest, uncomplaining and unafraid of hard work.

It was at Melchester Grammar School that he met 'Blackie' Gray, the fourth form captain. Like Roy, he belonged to Park House, and his nickname owed nothing to his surname and everything to his shock of black hair. He would become Roy's lifelong friend and confidant.

At one stage Roy became embroiled with Bert Beston, a nasty piece of work who, notwithstanding the presence of Blackie Gray and Roy, believed himself to be the best footballer at the school. On once particular occasion Beston deliberately charged into Roy in the art room, sending him crashing into a table covered with paint and drying artwork. It was multi-coloured carnage but the phlegmatic Roy took all the blame himself, and quietly got on with the job of cleaning up while the others enjoyed a pick-up game of football.

Beston was a constant pest. On another occasion he viciously stamped on Roy's right foot in an attempt to disrupt his blossoming schoolboy career, a move which backfired badly – Roy just trained harder with his left foot, turning himself into a player as adept on the pitch with his left foot as he was with his right, which put him in good stead for the years ahead.

Not content to stop there, the wretched Beston then tried to sabotage Roy's debut in the School's under-fifteen side by deliberately giving him the wrong directions to the away ground at Mosswick School. Roy's father was driving Roy, Blackie and two of the team's substitutes down to the match, and Beston's beastly trick meant that they only arrived just before half-time, with Melchester Grammar 3-0 down. Roy and Blackie soon set about the opposition, though, with Roy the former scoring the first of many illustrious hat-tricks and Blackie netting the winner.

In 1954, during a game for Milston (his youth club's football team) he came to the attention of Alf Leeds, a first division talent spotter for the Melchester Rovers A team. His match-winning performance impressed Alf, who invited Roy and Blackie to play for Melchester. The pair quickly developed an almost telepathic understanding of each other's game on the pitch, and that December, latching on to a perfectly weighted pass from Blackie, Roy scored his first 'senior' goal for Melchester Rovers.

His fifth year end-of-term report offers a snap shot of the young Roy Race. Though revealing an unsuspected aptitude for maths, and in particular algebra and trigonometry, his form master goes on to observe that, 'Roy's lack of interest in all matters scientific, except the annual field trip, must be reversed.'

English literature was a struggle and he 'needed to be motivated to keep up with his studies, especially with the English classics and Shakespeare,' but in English language there was a surprising revelation: 'Roy has demonstrated the ability to eloquently transcribe his thoughts into poetry and has shown an affinity for essay writing.' Melchester fans would definitely argue that some of his subsequent goals were almost lyrical and *real* works of art.

As for physical education: 'A most athletic young man, Roy has shown an aptitude for all sports … in the past few months he has shown an immense improvement in his football skills and would seem at his happiest with a ball at his feet. A most valuable member of the School First Eleven.'

The report concluded: 'Roy must be persuaded not to let the sporting side of his nature exclude the more important aspects of his study. He has shown himself to be a very personable young fellow, well-liked by his classmates, and capable of taking discipline as well as showing leadership qualities.'

Clearly he was a very personable and presentable young man, but equally nobody's fool and certainly not an individual to back down when the going got tough. In his very first year in the Melchester team – 1955 – he had the courage to square up to Arty Hedlow, Melchester's ten-thousand-pound record signing from Elbury

ROY CONTINUED TO FUNK AGAINST BIG RON BLAKE....

OOF!

ROY CRASHED TO THE GROUND, BADLY SHAKEN, BUT HE WASN'T BEATEN, YET

IF I CAN JUST--GET MY BOOT TO THE BALL-- HEDLOW'S WAITING-- UNMARKED!

EVEN AS BLAKE WAS ABOUT TO CLEAR THE BALL, ROY JUST MANAGED TO PUSH IT TO HEDLOW WITH A DESPERATE LUNGE

Wanderers, who had not only taken Blackie Gray's place in the side but then also accused Roy of hogging the ball!

As if!

'I'd like to knock your thundering block off' fumed Roy as he went

FULL TIME CAME BEFORE THE GAME COULD RESTART, AND THE VICTORIOUS ROVERS TROTTED DELIGHTEDLY OFF THE FIELD

WELL DONE, ROY! I NEVER THOUGHT WE'D DO IT! IT WAS THE TOUGHEST GAME WE'VE PLAYED THIS SEASON!

YOU'RE TELLING ME, BLACKIE! BUT WE'D NEVER HAVE WON IF PIERRE HADN'T BEEN PLAYING!

MA FOI! YOU PRAISE ME TOO 'IGH, ROY! YOU WON ZE GAME--NOT ME!

MODEST IN VICTORY
Roy's flash of genius after being floored had undoubtedly won the game for Melchester, but he preferred to heap praise on others.

ROY WAS TYPIFIED BY HIS NEVER-SAY-DIE ATTITUDE
Even when Roy was taken out by big Ron Blake and sent crashing to the ground his natural ability shone though. He managed to poke out his right foot to make a pass setting up a team-mate to score.

to grab Hedlow, only to be pulled back by captain Andy McDonald. 'Sooner or later the others will find out what a rotter you are.'

Being Roy, however, he was able to put his personal grievances aside on the pitch, and he set Hedlow up for the winning goal late in the second half. As ever, football, and Melchester Rovers, ultimately came first.

Roy was an overnight sensation. His unstoppable left-footed pile drivers, taken from twenty-five yards or more, gained them the nickname 'Rockets' and became the stuff of legend, feared around England's League grounds and ensuring he was voted Rovers' 'Young Player of the Year'. Hedlow, though an unpleasant man, also continued to demand media attention by scoring twenty-six goals in twenty-four games before a serious knee injury – this was before microsurgery and carbon grafts – ended his career prematurely.

There was never a dull moment at Melchester and in August 1956 Rovers signed the French winger Pierre Dupont from Rochemont, initially on a short trial. The signing angered Rover's right winger Sam Higby, who tried to ensure Pierre missed an important League match against Portdean City by luring him to take a relaxing stroll to the local lighthouse on the morning of the game, and promptly locking him in when he got there. He and Roy, who had had a newspaper blow into his face in the first half just as he was lining up a shot at goal, ensured nonetheless that Rovers won.

With Roy as their trump card, Rovers were on the march and in 1957 they claimed fourth place in the League, their highest ever position, which heralded their first championship triumph the following season. Their success that season was a fitting send-off for captain Andy McDonald who subsequently retired.

FAREWELL ANDY

Roy put together a scrapbook of press cuttings and photos when Melchester captain Andy MacDonald retired.

CAPTAINCY MATERIAL

Hughie Griffiths succeeded McDonald as captain in 1958 but after four defeats in a row he suffered a long-term knee injury – and despite his tender years, Roy was asked to stand-in. The captaincy was soon confirmed as permanent, and Roy's response must rank as one of the most clichéd ever: 'I'm chuffed. I feel like Sputnik, over the moon!' Not an awful lot of poetry there for his old English master to enthuse over.

GOOD TRIUMPHS

Ted Smith tried to sabotage Melchester's Cup run but Roy was equal to the challenge and led the team to victory at Wembley. Smith ended up in prison.

His first match as captain ended in a 3-3 draw against the League leaders Bamford Athletic and featured two new signings who were soon to become household names – goalkeeper Tubby Morton and right winger Dick Stokes. The League was clearly a write-off, but Rovers were growing in strength and confidence by the week and they went on to win the FA Cup, beating Langton United 3-2 with Roy scoring the winner in the dying seconds. Along the way Roy scored two successive hat-tricks – one in the fifth round away to Carnbrook Town and again in the sixth round at home to Bronton City.

In the fourth round Roy decided, as captain and without reference to coach or manager – in those days you could make up your own mind_ that he would swap Morton and Stokes. The move paid off. The keeper set up one goal and his stand-in another. Roy scored fourteen goals in that campaign from the third round to the final, scoring at least two goals a game alongside those two hat-tricks. It was a purple patch to match any in his career.

The FA Cup final took an intriguing turn when Ted Smith, formerly chauffeur to the Rovers chairman John Mason, attempted to sabotage their march to victory. When Smith cast Roy and Blackie adrift at sea in a dinghy off the coastal town of Portsea the ever-resourceful duo, with the pragmatic Roy displaying surprisingly acute nautical skills, made their way safely back to dry land. Smith was later arrested. Before the semi-final against Brampton United Roy had also had to rally the troops after a nasty accident involving the team coach on the way to the ground. There is no record of him having been a Boy Scout, but Baden Powell would have purred with delight.

The entire season had been incident-packed. In December Roy fought hard to clear Blackie's name when he was accused of arson after the Melchester Park stadium dressing rooms burned down during the Christmas break. He was forced to suspend Blackie from the team, and Ken Harcombe was signed up as replacement. Initially, the other players suspected him of being the real arsonist, but Roy's dogged investigations led him to believe others were responsible.

At half time in a match against the German team Flaudermitz, Roy realised to his horror that police officers had arrived at the ground intending to arrest Blackie. As the handcuffs began to appear, Roy 'accidentally' kicked a ball hard at one of the policemen – and not just any old kick, one of his left-footed rockets! In the

ROY CLEARS BLACKIE'S NAME AND EXPOSES THE REAL VILLAIN
Roy never believed that Blackie Gray had tried to burn down Melchester Stadium and set about discovering the real culprit – a local builder and robber Reg Murphy, who had started the fire while trying to recover stolen booty.

ensuing confusion, he grabbed Blackie and ran down into the ruined dressing rooms where they spotted Reg Murphy, a local builder busily up to no good with a spade in his hand. Startled, he promptly attacked Roy, spade aloft, but Roy retaliated with a 'whipcrack uppercut'. All became clear when it emerged that Murphy was digging in search of a box containing 'thousands of quid in notes and silver' – proceeds from the Melchester National Bank robbery that he and his accomplice, Mike Drury, had pulled off some years ago. Justice was served and, most importantly for Roy's peace of mind, Blackie was totally vindicated. Not that Roy had ever doubted him for a second.

In February 1960 Roy was in boy scout survival mode again when the Transatlantic Air Services plane carrying Rovers to San Angino in South America for their International Club cup-tie crash-landed on the island of Beltigua and vanished off all radar screens. The plane had been shot down by rebel forces. Roy and his Rovers had to march through jungle and swamp until they eventually emerged into a clearing in the forest to find, of all things, a football pitch! Roy was at his stoical best and the Rovers played two matches against a rebel team which left them bruised, battered and bewildered – but alive.

On their return to Melchester they were allowed to defer five League games in order to try to recover from their ordeal, but by May they were up and at 'em again, and en route to Portdean City for the Championship decider. The match was broadcast live on Radio Melchester, a novelty in those days when local radio was in its infancy. Rovers won the match, and the Championship, with Roy sending a penalty kick swerving into the top right-hand corner of the net, while the Portdean keeper Ernie Wilson took a costly dive to his left.

The Rovers' South American jaunts – obviously financially re- warding for Melchester – were always fraught in the extreme, and there were more to come. Four years later, in August 1964, the team were kidnapped in the republic of Malagos, where they had flown to play a World Club Cup game against local side Bagota. After enjoying a lavish presidential welcome they went on to their training

WHAT A GOAL!
Roy scored some absolute gems in his long career. The overhead volley, such as this one against Bagota, became something of a speciality and often proved a match-winning weapon.

KIDNAPPED IN MALAGOS

Local brigands proved Melchester's stiffest opposition, but the South American tour ended with a 17-2 victory.

ground in the hills, where local brigands took them hostage. Rovers were obliged to demonstrate their skills in a match against the rebels. Unsurprisingly, Rovers won by a staggering 17-2 before escaping on horseback through the Amazonian jungle, arriving with minutes left before the kick-off against Bagota after forty-eight hours without sleep! Luckily, two of the rebels who had befriended them, Bruno and Beppo, slipped the team some of the local 'carioca' juice at half-time. Chances are that 'carioca' juice was cocaine-based, something Roy would have never endorsed, but ignorance is bliss – Rovers played like men possessed and went on to win the game!

Domestically, the 1960-61 season had seen an unexpected challenge from Shermall Athletic, the 'other' club in Melchester, who had been promoted from the Second Division. Roy the 'poet' wasn't at his sparkling best when asked to comment by the local rag: 'We can't sit back on our laurels nor will we count our chickens before they come home to roost.' Just as well he could play a bit given his lamentable performances in press conferences.

Rovers were without a win in the first six games, managing just three draws and finding themselves one rung away from relegation. Shermall, meanwhile, had won all six of their opening fixtures. There was a lot to prove as they headed into the local derby. Roy was at his best under pressure, though, and Rovers emerged as the 4-1 victors with Roy scoring a hat-trick, netting the third while he was acting goalkeeper.

There was further drama for Rovers in November 1960 when the Shermall chairman Lance Vigors sensationally bought them after John Mason's department store empire ran into financial difficulties. Rovers and Shermall Athletic then swapped grounds. Rovers lost their first game at their new home, the 4-1 defeat their biggest for five years. Granted, Shermall Stadium was luxuriously appointed, Vigors having spared no expense in turning Athletic into a top-flight club and ground, but it wasn't home for the Rovers team or their fans. For one thing it lacked the distinctive smell of pickled onions from the pickling factory next door to their beloved Melchester Park!

A mystery fire at Shermall Stadium in January 1961 forced them to move back to Mel Park for a third round FA Cup tie. They had to win if Roy was to stay at the club after failing to see eye to eye with Vigors. Roy scored the only goal of the match and they reached the semi-finals where, would you credit it, they were drawn at home to … Shermall Athletic! Roy was subjected to a little rough treatment

because he was suspected – without any grounds, of course – of being involved in the kidnap of two Athletic players. But he scored the equaliser before half time and added a second after the break as Rovers ended up the 3-1 winners.

The final in May 1961 was against Corstone City. Rovers went one down but Roy equalised courtesy of an assist from centre half Don Pike, the local sports reporter who could also 'play a bit'. Sadly in setting Roy up for that goal, Pike injured a knee that was ultimately to threaten his career. Nevertheless, he somehow managed climb up to the press box where he immediately started typing peerless running copy for his boss at the *Daily Gazette*. Roy scored the winner of course but he was already looking ahead to the relegation fight. To avoid relegation they had to win their last two league matches by five clear goals – and they did precisely that.

THEY ALSO SERVED

Simply by virtue of his extraordinary performance on the pitch and impact on the game, Roy invariably grabbed all the headlines throughout his long career. But he was also the ultimate team man and it it is only right that proper tribute be paid to his many team-mates, many of them outstanding players in their own right:

Noel Baxter, Gary Bracken, Karl Bruckner, Charlie 'The Cat' Carter, Trevor Cassidy, Kevin Clark, Jeff Cooper, Matt Croker, Paco Diaz, Johnny 'The Hard Man' Dexter, Pierre Dupont, Keith Durham, Vernon Eliot, Paul Evans, Craig Foster, Geoff Giles, Ralph 'Flash' Gordon, Nat 'Grandad' Gosden, Blackie Gray, Anton Gronvold, Vic Guthrie, Nick 'Rapper' Hardisty, Emlyn 'Crazy Horse' Hughes, Carl Hunt, Nevill Jones, Martin Kemp, Andy Kerrigan, Ritchie Lawrence, Kenny Logan, Duncan Mckay, Declan McKaffree, Bruce 'Pancho'Miller, Tubby Morton, Derek 'Mozzie' Mostin, Jamie Nash, Steve Naylor, Steve Norman, Olaf 'Olly' Olsen, Jimmy Slade, Andy 'Streaky' Styles, Dion Templeton, Mervyn Wallace, Bob 'Clean Sheet King' Wilson, Steve 'Nobby' Wooten.

ENGLAND BECKONS

By 1962 Mel Park had been given a much needed makeover, though nothing could ever expunge the smell of pickled onions, and the Italian giants Stadia Batori had made an unsuccessful eighty-five-thousand-pound offer for Roy who showed no interest in moving. Rovers played their first European Cup Winners' Cup match against Schonved of Hungary, but lost 2-1 after a strange incident during which the ball burst on its way into the goal for an equaliser. It simply never got there. In a season of solid consolidation, Rovers finished mid-table and lost in the fifth round of FA Cup.

By April 1963 the England selectors were belatedly taking note and arrived en masse to watch Roy in a league match against Eastoke United. Roy was unusually nervous, and fluffed a few early chances, but he recovered to score a hat-trick in the second half – all with his head, which was gratifying after working hard in training with a new heading machine. He then finished magnificently by hammering home a fourth goal with his right foot. The home crowd went wild but, ever the perfectionist, it was his missed chances in the first half that Roy fretted about. Nevertheless, he was named as centre forward when the England squad was announced the following Thursday. He celebrated by scoring seventeen goals in his next six games as Rovers stepped up their challenge for League honours.

His England debut against Caragua started badly with Roy distracted by thoughts of how Melchester Rovers were doing in their match that same afternoon against title rivals Wellingbury. Roy was worried for his friend and team mate Tom Dawson, who had been told that he would face the sack if his form didn't improve.

As soon as Roy had been informed that Rovers were leading and that Dawson had scored, the mood lightened at once. With the shackles off he promptly scored a stunning goal on debut with a thunderous volley. He also claimed England's second and third goals with a dazzling solo effort as they finished 3-1 winners. With Roy in such form, Rovers unsurprisingly went on to win the League Championship.

DIFFICULT ENGLAND DEBUT
Roy was worried about how Melchester were doing against Wellingbury in the League but recovered to score a sensational second-half hat-trick.

Rovers were in the European Cup for the first time the following season and Roy scored six goals on their way to the final in Paris against Italian side Nettruno. That's when the fun *really* began. Blackie Gray and Ed Garrard both fell in love with the sexy French film actress Suzanne Cerise. The rivalry began a feud between the two players, which looked for a while like it might jeopardise the match; but thankfully they managed to put their jealousies aside for the sake of the team. They made it to the final just in time to play (this late arrival of key players, often Roy himself, was a recurring theme throughout this period) but Rovers quickly went 1-0 down after Roy made a bad call in deciding to play into a fierce wind. Bad turned to worse, and by half-time Rovers had conceded a second

TAKE THAT! ROY OPENS HIS ACCOUNT FOR ENGLAND
On hearing that all was going well for Melchester against Wellingbury and that his friend Tom Dawson, who had been threatened with the sack, was enjoying a blinder, Roy relaxed and celebrated with the opening goal of his hat-trick.

ROY OF THE ROVERS – FRIEND OF THE STARS

Rovers were struggling in the European Cup Final in Paris, so Roy decided to perk his team up by arranging a half-time visit from 'sex bomb' film star Suzanne Cerise. She later married Ed Garrard, breaking Blackie's heart in the process.

goal. To save the day, Roy turned amateur psychologist and asked Suzanne Cerise to pay the players a visit in the changing room. She implored them to win for her, promising the players a surprise if they were victorious. One can only imagine what the tabloids would make of such a situation today! It did the trick, though. Roy scored twice in quick succession after the break and Blackie cracked in the winner. Rovers were the new European Champions. And the 'surprise' from Suzanne? Her post-match announcement that she and Ed Garrard were to marry. Blackie, grinning bravely through his misery, sportingly agreed to be best man.

In 1964, shortly after their second traumatic South American experience, Roy's Rovers signed the aristocrat and millionaire Lord D'arcy Plantagenet Trudgeon-Marclay, better known as 'Jumbo' Trudgeon. He played inside left and on his debut against Sandford Athletic he scored a hat-trick. A new cult figure was born.

By November, Rovers were top of the table and back at Melchester Park following yet another enforced absence from the ground when it had flooded. But, as ever, catastrophe was just around the corner. While playing a home game against Silford Athletic and leading 2-0, the ground dramatically subsided – taking with it their League chances. The match had to be abandoned, and although thankfully there were few serious injuries things were not looking good for the Rovers. That season, they bowed out of the

FA Cup in tears with a 4-3 defeat against Meltham Rangers in the semi-finals

The following year featured the good, the bad and the ugly. Rovers lost 1-0 to Norwegian part-timers Trondheim in the European Cup and crashed out of the League Cup with a sen-sational 2-1 defeat against Fourth Division Midbury Town. Salvation, however, came in the final of the FA Cup where they beat Eastoke United the League Champions 2-1, Roy heading the winner despite playing with a dodgy knee.

STRANGE HAPPENINGS AT MELCHESTER

Anything could happen in the footballing world of Roy of the Rovers. Here a vital league game was called off after sudden subsidence at the ground. Thankfully nobody was injured. The cause remained a mystery for many years.

ROY THE CHOIRMASTER

Although he was teetotal Roy enjoyed the boot-room cameraderie as much as the next man, especially the long coach journeys home from away matches or foreign trips.

Drawing on the 'poetic skills' that his old school form master spotted in him at an early age, he occasionally penned specially adapted versions of the Melchester team song, which was always sung to the tune of 'Waltzing Matilda'. That's when he wasn't belting out his own personal renditions of his favourite Victor Damone classics, 'This Game of Love' and 'That Towering Feeling'.

The first such recorded instance of Roy's songwriting prowess was during Blackie Gray's birthday party, with reserve team captain Phil Finnigan, a popular Irishman, backing Roy on his accordion:

> Who'd play the Rovers,
> Who'd play the Rovers,
> Who'd play the Rovers, at home or away ...?
> And the goalkeeper cried, as his crossbar fell on top of him,
> That was a sizzler from old Blackie Gray!

Inside left Jim Hallett sometimes used to strike up on his harmonica and the next recorded version came on their way back from an annual charity match at Cliffport United when he also added the words:

> Who'd play the Rovers,
> Who'd play the Rovers,
> Who'd play the Rovers, and still stand the pace!
> And the goalkeeper groaned, as a supersonic ball flew by,
> That makes a hat-trick for old Roy Race!"

In the summer of 1956, French right winger Pierre Dupont was on trial with the Rovers and he struck up a great friendship with Roy and Blackie. One afternoon Roy and his family were entertaining Pierre and they burst into the Rovers tune with Penny leading the way on the piano:

> Who'd play the Rovers,
> Who'd play the Rovers,
> Who'd play the Rovers, with Pierre on our wing?
> And the left back declared, as a cannonball in shorts flew by,
> That flying Frenchman can move with a zing!

In the summer of 1957, Rovers were on tour in Canada and were due to play a team called Macey's Bluff, in the Western settlements among the foothills of the Rocky Mountains. Roy's adaptation on that occasion went thus:

> Who'd play the Rovers,
> Who'd play the Rovers,
> Who'd play the Rovers, they're all mighty tough!
> And the Canuck groaned, as the poor old goalie bit the dust,
> 'Those durn tootin' Rovers have called Macey's Bluff!'

And finally – you can only take so much of this stuff – the summer of 1959 saw the Rovers on tour in Italy and they had bought Jim Hallett a red accordion for his birthday.. Again to the tune of 'Waltzing Matilda' and accompanied by Jim, they went for broke and produced a new verse, as well as the chorus!

> Once a jolly soccer team toured on the Continent,
> Under the scorching Italian sun;
> But they said when the heat began to melt their soccer boots,
> We'll keep a-fighting until we have won!
>
> Who'd play the Rovers,
> Who'd play the Rovers,
> Who'd play the Rovers, at home or abroad?
> As the sweat from their brows ran down and cooled their
>   shooting boots,
> Well played the grease-spots, the Rovers had scored!

TRAGEDY

Tragedy struck for Roy late in 1966 when Melchester lost their two defenders Dave Williams and Bob Roberts in a crash at a charity speedway event. The rookies who replaced them – Ken Cooper and Derek Millar – took time to settle in and Rovers understandably struggled in the League. But they triumphed gloriously in the European Cup Winners' Cup, during which Roy introduced the then revolutionary man-on-man marking system in the semi-final against Spanish side Real Corbao. The final was against Portuguese side Sporting Alcero and was staged at Hampden Park, Glasgow. Rovers nicked it 2-1 and after such a morale boosting victory they went on to destroy Melborough 7-0 to avoid relegation in the League.

In March 1968 Roy scored his 300th goal, a club record. In the climax to the season Roy was carried off but manager Ben Galloway refused to send on a sub, hoping that Roy might yet be able to return. And of course Roy does return, knowing that victory against Highwood Athletic, who began the match a point ahead of Rovers,

would give Melchester the League title. When Jumbo was knocked unconscious in a collision, substitute Alec Blackburn came on and scored the winner, from Roy's pass, to claim a staggering fourth League title in ten years for Melchester.

The European Cup provided the greatest excitement of 1969, when they beat Leonardo of Italy in the semi-finals on the away goal rule. Once again they faced a final in Paris, against the Portuguese champions Santova Rapid. Just before the game, Blackie Gray sustained a nasty injury after a horse kicked him in the head. This was aggravated when he suffered a clash of heads at a corner. Surely severely concussed at this point, Roy's best mate seized the ball on halfway and dribbled past six or seven defenders to score a cracking goal – unfortunately, against Rovers! Nonetheless, they managed to hang on for a 3-1 win.

They flew direct from Paris to Mexico for a summer tour. For once their visit to the South American continent was free of alarm and trauma, really almost boring in comparison to their previous visits.

In 1971 Roy and his Rovers won the Cup Winners' Cup beating the Belgian side Standard Wasserdam. The win was celebrated the following day with a civic reception and a ride in an open-top bus through the streets of Melchester. Roy's thirteen goals in the European campaign was a record for a British player in all three European competitions. And he also finished that season as England's top scorer with 48 goals; the fifth year on the trot he had been top marksman.

The club's former player Tony Storme returned to Melchester in 1972 and guided them to the European Cup, defeating the Portuguese side Carados 2-0 while Roy and Blackie enjoyed one of their high spots as an England duo scoring a goal apiece in a splendid 2-0 England win over Italy.

The 1973-74 season proved to be a challenging one both psychologically and physically. To start with Roy was shot in the leg by Colonel Chadwick while trying to quell a demonstration against a local bypass scheme that Jumbo Trudgeon had become embroiled in. The injury was not quite as bad as he at first feared and a determined Roy managed to keep his time out of the game to a minimum.

In the FA Cup final that year, Rovers director Ted Manning offered a tempting £7,000 bonus per man per goal but, to Manning's surprise, Roy was furious at the offer. He was a man of principle and

ROVERS' TEAM FOR THE EUROPEAN CUP FINAL

1 TUBBY MORTON
2 DEREK MILLAR
3 KEN COOPER
4 GEOFF GILES
5 ANDY CROYDON
6 LOFTY PEAK
7 TERRY WEST
8 BLACKIE GRAY
9 ROY RACE
10 JUMBO TRUDGEON
11 TOM DAWSON
12 CHRIS DYLAN

ROY RACE WAS SKIPPER OF MELCHESTER ROVERS, WHO HAD REACHED THE FINAL OF THE EUROPEAN CUP. THEY WERE PLAYING THE FINAL IN FRANCE, AGAINST THE PORTUGUESE CHAMPIONS, SANTOVA RAPID. ROVERS' INSIDE-RIGHT BLACKIE GRAY HAD JUST MADE A BRILLIANT RUN, BUT IN THE WRONG DIRECTION. HE SEEMED UNAWARE THAT HE WAS ABOUT TO SCORE A GOAL FOR SANTOVA.

BLACKIE'S SCORED FOR THE OPPOSITION!

BLACKIE, WHAT HAPPENED?

HE DOESN'T SEEM TO KNOW WHAT YOU'RE TALKING ABOUT. IT MUST BE THAT BASH ON THE HEAD HE GOT!

SUDDENLY —

HE'S GONE OUT LIKE A LIGHT!

BLACKIE'S BADLY HURT, REF. CAN WE HAVE OUR TRAINER ON?

TAFFY MORGAN HAD BLACKIE TAKEN OFF AND REPLACED BY SUB CHRIS DYLAN.

felt strongly that the unique Cup double was the only thing that mattered and should be incentive enough for the players – the money would prove a distraction.

His reaction underlined what has been apparent throughout his life and his career. It was football that mattered, not the money involved, something that would make him almost unique today. Roy was no materialist. Throughout his dealings with Melchester there was not even a hint of any disagreement over money. Roy was just as unselfish off the pitch as he was on it. He was pragmatic about the gifts that came his way, simply accepting them with grace and not using them to glorify himself or distance himself from his team-mates or from the fans.

A League Cup and FA Cup double helped stuff the trophy cabinet full to groaning in 1974, but how the mighty fell the following season. Rovers crashed out of the FA Cup to non-League Sleeford Town, after having a goal disallowed. Manager Tony Storme had signed a circus juggler, Sammy Spangler, as a replacement for the injured Jumbo Trudgeon, but the rest of the players considered him unreliable and team spirit tumbled. Rovers were not doing well in the League either, and after the FA Cup defeat Storme did a runner and disappeared. Roy was offered the post of player-manager, which, after a diplomatic delay to give Storme time to reappear and explain himself – there were fears he had suffered a nervous breakdown – he accepted.

I'M NOT SURE IF YOU ARE CHEERING BECAUSE I'VE JUST EARNED YOU ANOTHER TWO THOUSAND POUNDS, OR BECAUSE WE'RE BACK IN WITH A GOOD CHANCE OF PULLING OFF THE CUP DOUBLE...!

AS FAR AS I'M CONCERNED, ALL THAT MATTERS IS WINNING THE CUP... WHICH MEANS *STOPPING BURNDEAN*, AS WELL AS SCORING GOALS!

ROY TAKES OVER AS MANAGER

Given his background it was no surprise, surely, that Rovers turned to Roy in their moment of need. But like many others who have found themselves in similar positions he initially tried to be all things to all men and ended up losing focus. It all seemed to be going badly wrong as they trailed 2-0 to lowly Castledene in his opening game. Roy was at a loss, until a middle-aged man, apparently a Castledene fan, slipped Roy a note suggesting, 'stop fussing like a mother hen and get on with your own game.' Roy took the hint and led his side to an encouraging win. It would later transpire that the mystery fan had, in fact, been Tony Storme, in disguise but still rooting for his boys from the sidelines.

After that they went from strength to strength, Roy never again shirking from tough decisions. In the European Cup Winners' Cup final, against Greek side Niarkos at Hampden Park, he substituted his good friend Lofty Peak, Melchester's best defender, in a late gamble which paid off handsomely. The following season started superbly with Melchester breaking their record, dating back to 1957-58, of going undefeated for nineteen matches in the League. However, although they were playing exciting football not even Melchester could win all of the time and their League campaign fell away disappointingly.

Happier days were just around the corner though. After losing the FA Cup final to a controversial refereeing decision – did the ball cross the line for a Rovers goal or not? – Roy finally got married to the raven-haired beauty Penny, Ben Galloway's secretary. This was some twenty-one years into his football career and he was nearing

TACTICAL MASTERSTROKE
Substituting their best player on the night offered Niarkos the bait.

his thirty-ninth birthday, proving that thus far he really had been married to football … and some habits die hard, it seems: he broke off from his honeymoon in Italy to appear for a European Select Eleven against a South America Eleven in a pre-1976-77 season tournament in Brazil. He also rushed back from his honeymoon to score as England defeated France 3-0 to win the European Nations Cup, the only major honour he won with England.

NOTHING LIKE A GOOD CELEBRATION

Roy made light of the pressure of being player-manager at one of England's top clubs, but occasionally he let off steam when they landed the big trophies and enjoyed a lap of honour as much as the next man.

THE WEDDING OF THE YEAR

HELLO! magazine wasn't around then, but public interest in Roy's wedding to the beautiful raven-haired Penny — Ben Galloway's secretary — was intense. Roy celebrated by shooting an autographed football into the crowd.

THE JOYS OF FATHERHOOD!
Roy was looking forward to becoming a father, but the arrival of twins was a shock.

final of the European Cup only to lose to Alkhoven of Holland, to the great delight of a number of their inter-national contingent who saw it as revenge for their country's humili-ation earlier in the season.

In the 1978-79 season Rovers reached the final of the UEFA Cup, in the run-up to which Roy was greatly impressed by the Spanish right winger Paco Diaz, Spain's greatest ever player in the eyes of some. In May that year Roy plunged into the transfer market and signed Diaz for £700,000, although he wouldn't be eligible to play until the second leg of the final – rather strange as you would assume he would have been cup-tied altogether. As he considered his options he reluctantly dropped winger Merv Wallace but such were Roy's man management skills that he conjured a match-winning perform-ance from Wallace when he came on as substitute in the second leg, though predictably it was Roy who netted the winning goal.

ENGLAND OUR ENGLAND
Nothing could ever match the pride and joy of playing for and captaining England.

As night follows day, Roy was appointed caretaker manager of England for a friendly against Holland in January 1978 after the incumbent was injured in a car accident. Roy included no fewer than six of his Melchester players in the squad but opted for an exciting twin strike force up front – Birmingham's Trevor Francis and Malcolm 'SuperMac' MacDonald, then of Arsenal. The result was truly spectacular – the team won 5-1 over the highly rated Dutch with a hat-trick for Francis and two for SuperMac. Roy ordered champagne for the boys that night – he was teetotal himself. Not everything went his way that season, though. Rovers reached the

ROY OF THE ROVERS PROFILE – <u>WOMEN'S</u> MAGAZINE 1977

Full name: Roy Race.

Birthplace: Melchester.

Height: 6 ft 2 in.

Weight: 12 st 3 lb.

Married: Yes, to Penny.

Children: Twins, Roy Jr and Melinda (born in May 1977 on the day Rovers won the Championship and Roy handed credit for the fiftieth goal to his team mate Mervyn Wallace).

Favourite car: Lotus Elan.

Favourite food: Trifle and smoked salmon (although not together).

Favourite drink: Hot, strong tea (I'm 'tea'total).

Favourite match: First match for Rovers in 1955, and first game for England in 1963.

Biggest disappointment: Not playing more for England.

Best goal: All 400+ of them.

Favourite actor/actress: Paul Newman, Shirley Maclaine.

Favourite singers: Barbra Streisand, Vic Damone

Favourtie TV shows: *Monty Python's Flying Circus*, *Match of the Day* and *Quiz Ball*.

Favourite reading material: Sports pages and Melchester match programmes.

Ambitions: To stay fit and healthy, win more caps for England and ultimately play in the World Cup finals.

Which personality most like to meet: Pele.

Favourite sayings: 'If it isn't broke, why fix it?', 'Practice makes perfect.'.

NEVER LOOK A GIFT HORSE IN THE MOUTH

The fabulously rich Sheik of Basran wanted Roy to coach his struggling national side and was reluctant to take no for an answer. He showered riches on the Melchester man, but could Roy be bought?

THE BASRAN CONNECTION

In September 1979 the Sheikh of Basran offered Roy a million pounds – about the equivalent of about six million pounds today - to take over as soccer supremo, an offer he turned down although he and his wife Penny did fly out to Basran with the twins (now two years old). The uncertainty affected Rovers' early season form and after four games they were bottom of the First Division, Roy constantly being pestered by the Sheikh to reconsider, and losing his form in the upset. By December Rovers were still winless and struggling, and Roy was sacked as manager, although he continued as a player. Ben Galloway, sensing that this was just a temporary crisis, wisely promised that when Rovers won again, Roy would be reinstated.

Finally the drought broke when Melchester recorded a victory over the Russian side Dynamo Zarcov in the UEFA Cup – back to their winning ways, they went on to reach the final. It had been a difficult time for Roy and in the programme notes for their next league game, against Carford City, Roy gave it to the Melchester faithful straight:

> To put the record straight – I will not be accepting the million pound offer from Basran – I wouldn't leave Rovers for all the riches in the world. On the table was a palatial home, swimming pool, all the servants we wanted, luxury care – the works. But I have rejected them all. A representative from the Foreign Office visited me the other day. He urged me to take the job, said that the Sheikh might inflate the price of oil if I didn't! So, to the Sheikh, the British Government and to you all, I give the same message. I'm staying put.

He did, however, go to Basran to coach for the summer and to help set up the country's first football league, taking his wife and children with him. On returning from the summer consultancy, Roy found the Sheikh was still persistently trying to tempt him to work full-time. He sent Roy a Rolls Royce as a gift, which Roy rejected, auctioning it in aid of charity instead. In the end, Roy negotiated a compromise deal whereby Lofty Peak, whose Melchester contract has expired, would become the full-time national coach of Basran – an ideal solution for all concerned.

With Lofty's departure to the Middle East, the 1979-80 season saw Roy take the bold decision to replace him with Vic 'Superbrat' Guthrie, who repaid his player-manager's faith by settling in well. This was a prime example of Roy's shrewd handling of a player others had labelled 'difficult'. The season was best remembered for

KNOW YOUR OWN MIND

Playing football was the easy bit! As Roy was to discover, fighting the boardroom battles and internal club politics was what really stressed him. Rule number one: don't make any promises.

the second leg of the UEFA Cup-tie against Icelandic part-timers Heklavik when the Rovers squad were struck down by food poisoning. Roy had to bring in six reserves and use himself as a sub. But Heklavik scored to take an overall lead and Roy's last minute penalty was saved to seal their fate, a moment he considered to be the most humiliating in Melchester's entire history.

The following weeks and months were a huge test of Roy's managerial skills but the players responded superbly to haul themselves into the running for the League title. Roy, who was passionate about squash, rather unwisely played a vigorous game a few days before their sixth round FA Cup tie at Chalkford Town and, predictably, suffered an injury which saw him miss that match and watch his team suffer another calamitous defeat. A blazing row with

his chairman Sam Barlow about the injury ensued and Roy, sensing he was fighting for his managerial life, promised that Melchester would win the League.

Luckily, they did!

It all started to go wrong in the 1980-81 season when a lacklustre Rovers were relegation candidates throughout the campaign. Ultimately it all boiled down to the last match of the season when they had to defeat Stambridge City by five clear goals to stay up. Roy's side cam close, but fell agonisingly short with a magnificent 4-0 win.

But if Roy thought that was as calamitous as things could get, he was cruelly wrong.

WORLD ELEVEN

In the 1978 annual he lists his all-time World Eleven (it was restricted in fact to the previous ten years, with a couple of exceptions). Roy manages to include seven players from Britain!

Gordon Banks (England); **Giacinto Facchetti** (Italy), **Alf Ramsay**, **Jack Charlton, Bobby Moore, Bobby Charlton** (all England), **Franz Beckenbauer, Gunter Netzer** (both Germany), **Pele** (Brazil), **Denis Law** (Scotland), **George Best** (Northern Ireland).

WHO SHOT ROY OF THE ROVERS?

In December 1981 the soccer world was shocked to the core when Roy was shot and left for dead in his office by an unknown gunman. This was one in a long list of such high-profile assassination attempts, which had recently rocked the world. On 13 May 1981 there had been an unsuccessful attempt on the life of Pope John Paul in Rome, while two months earlier President Regan has been a target just seventy days after his inauguration. A year earlier, on 21 March 1980, the fictional murder of J. R. Ewing in *Dallas* had prompted the biggest on-screen murder hunt in TV history. To the close-knit football community of Melchester, Roy's assassination attempt and fight for life had no less impact.

There were five suspects:

1: **Arnie Meckiff:** A cousin from Australia whom Roy had threatened to turn over to the police when he discovered Meckiff's part in a crooked land share scheme.

2: **Vic Guthrie:** The 'Superbrat', who had been suspended for disciplinary reasons. It was Guthrie who had found Roy lying wounded in his office, only giving more reason to add him to the list.

3: **Trevor Brinsden:** An overly passionate Melchester fan who had been banned from all home games by Roy because of his part in causing disturbances on the terraces and outside the ground.

4: **Elton Blake:** An actor who had been sacked from playing the part of Roy Race – his big career break – in an upcoming TV soap series on Rovers and the exploits of its star player.

5: **Arthur Logan:** Father of Kenny Logan, who believed his son had been coerced by Roy to sign for Rovers instead of working for the family estate agency business.

LIKE LAZARUS HE ROSE FROM THE DEAD

The football world held its breath as Roy of the Rovers fought
for his life. The Melchester crowd chanted – louder and
louder – and in his hospital bed less than a mile away
Roy responded. Slowly he opened his eyes.
He was back with us!

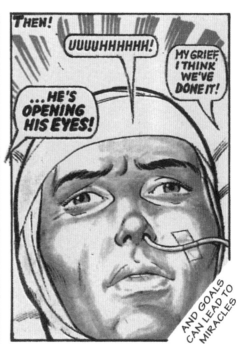

SIR ALF COMES TO THE RESCUE

Only one man could possibly step in for Roy as manager as our hero began his long recovery. England's World Cup-winning manager Sir Alf Ramsey was a stunning success during his caretaker spell at Melchester.

The last three suspects had all threatened revenge for their particular grievances, but for a while the investigation took a back seat as Roy fell into a coma and was put on the critical list at Melchester General Hospital where he remained throughout December and January. Although he was taken off the critical list at the beginning of February 1982 as his wounds healed, Roy remained in a coma, his wife Penny and their two children keeping a constant vigil at his bedside. The Rovers board did not believe that Roy would ever come out of the coma, and they appointed Sir Alf Ramsey, England's World Cup supremo of 1966, to the position of caretaker manager, safe in the knowledge that at a time of such heightened emotions he would handle the job with sensitivity.

Ramsey's second match in charge saw Rovers go 2-0 up and suddenly, of one accord, the fifty thousand assembled fans started to chant Roy's name, as one voice, louder and louder as if imploring him to wake from his coma. It was an extraordinarily poignant moment, and those of us who followed the story still recall it with tears in our eyes. At Roy's bedside, the doctors sensed the power of the moment and turned the volume up to maximum on the radio. Penny, tears pouring down her face, urged her husband to wake up.

All of a sudden, Roy opened his eyes. He was back.

The news was quickly conveyed to the ground and read out by an emotional tannoy announcer. Both the teams, and all the fans, celebrated wildly. Roy was the most popular man in English football. He was alive. He would play again. A super-charged Rovers went on a joyous goal-spree and were 7-0 up against Keysborough when Roy uttered his first words: 'What's the record for the most goals scored by one team in a Football League game, Penny?'

The answer came from a fan in an adjacent ward, and was relayed by a doctor: 'It's thirteen by Newcastle, Stockport and Tranmere.' Rovers were 8-0 ahead at this point, prompting Roy to say: 'So Rovers need another six to break the record.' His words were conveyed to the ground and the match ended with a fourteenth and final goal hammered home by Rovers in the final minute, a record-breaking finish to a quite astonishingly eventful game.

Roy was discharged from hospital at the end of February, his assailant still unknown and still at large. Sir Alf stayed in charge throughout March, during which Rovers stretched their unbeaten run to thirty-four games, and by the beginning of April Roy was back at work after Ramsey's excellent stint as caretaker manager.

During his playing comeback match against Hunterford in May, Roy scored the first two goals of the 3-0 win. At half-time, he suddenly took himself off the pitch; in a flash of inspiration, he had realised the identity of his would-be assassin. He left the ground in a hurry and travelled directly to Melchester police station to present evidence that led to the arrest of … the actor Elton Blake.

ROY'S RETURN AS A PLAYER WAS LONG-ANTICIPATED

Roy was naturally keen to resume playing as soon as possible — indeed that, determination underpinned his recovery — but when the moment finally came he was understandably nervous.

SUDDENLY A FLASHBACK REVEALED ALL

With his mind racing as kick-off time approached, Roy suddenly recalled everything about the horrific shooting incident he had pushed to the back of his mind.

THE MOMENT OF TRUTH

Roy confronted the former television star Elton Blake, and before long he had confessed to everything.

MARITAL STRIFE

The birth of their third child, Diana (named after the Princess of Wales, who had married Prince Charles the previous year) appeared to herald a much-deserved period of domestic happiness, after the traumas of the shooting. But for Roy, as for the rest of us, sometimes life doesn't work out as planned.

By November, two squabbling twins and a demanding baby began to take their toll on Roy. He felt under pressure and deprived of sleep; he was tired at work and irritable at home. His unhappiness was evident to one and all. At a meeting to discuss plans for the revamp of Mel Park Roy dozed off at the table but, typically, still managed to point out that the proposed new leisure centre would block the fans' access to the River Stand – so back to the drawing board.

Things started to stack up against him. There were even fans demonstrating outside his house, demanding that he drop Tubby

LIFE WAS TURNING SOUR FOR THE GOLDEN BOY!
On top of his player-manager duties with Melchester, Roy was discovering, being a father to three young children was very tiring indeed. He started to fall asleep at inopportune times.

ROY IS MADE AN OFFER HE CAN'T REFUSE
Melchester fans were unhappy when Roy dropped Tubby Morton, the club directors were interfering and things at home were difficult. Harvey Rawson sensed Roy's discontent and made an attractive offer for him to join their arch rivals Walford Rovers.

THE PRESSURE GROWS

Penny was a Melchester girl through and through, and although the offer from Walford was lucrative she was very unhappy at the prospect of Roy quitting 'her' club.

Morton and reinstate their old keeper Charlie 'The Cat' Carter, or else resign.

When Walford's new chairman Harvey Rawson offered Roy £3,000 per week and £5 million pounds to spend on players, everyone assumed Roy would reject it, as he had all the others, because of his unswerving loyalty to Melchester. But by early March Roy felt he was being taken for granted – even Penny, a Melchester girl remember, did not take the Walford offer seriously. To exacerbate things the Board and players alike were questioning all his decisions. So he did the unthinkable. He quit for Walford.

Penny and the children stayed in Melchester, and in anger she took the children on holiday to Crete, a very public separation for one of Britain's most high-profile couples. He also received hate mail from Melchester fans, and the media coverage if anything intensified in August when Roy was photographed in all the newspapers with a gorgeous blonde at a Walford supporters' club dance.

In fact Roy was innocent, she was his secretary Sandie Lewis though he should have known better than to be photographed with her. By September an irate Penny had returned from Crete and went straight to Melchester, believing the worst in the wake of the Sandie Lewis story. Midlife or otherwise, Roy was in crisis, and the situation was badly affecting his football game, though he did rouse himself to

THE UNTHINKABLE BECOMES REALITY

Roy eventually went against everybody's advice and signed for Walford – and ironically he was soon leading out his new club against . . . Melchester.

CAN THIS REALLY BE HAPPENING?
Walford understandably milked the publicity value of their incredible new signing for all it was worth, and Harvey Rawson himself welcomed the legendary Roy Race onto the ground.

produce a man of the match performance when Walford defeated Rovers.

Meanwhile, Blackie Gray had been installed as manager at Melchester and brought Rob Richards into the First Eleven. Dubbed 'Superkid', Richards bore an uncanny resemblance to Roy Race and was hailed as 'the new Roy of the Rovers', so much so that Gray felt able to sell Paco Diaz on to Real Varagossa.

Roy meanwhile was going from bad to worse. He wanted to get back together with Penny, and something had to give. Realising where Roy's loyalties lay, Harvey Rawson very decently released him from his contract. Roy returned to Melchester as player-manager. How happy Blackie was to stand down, we will never know. But Melchester certainly responded well, and they immediately picked up form to reach the final of the FA Cup where, in a twist of fate, they met Walford. A loaded match that Melchester won 2-1.

The 1984-85 season was a golden time starting, unexpectedly,

WHY IS THAT MYSTERY BLONDE DRIVING ROY'S CAR?
The media camp out at Walford's ground and their suspicions are aroused when an attractive blonde arrives in Roy's distinctive Lotus sports car. It was the club secretary Sandie Lewis, and she had picked it up for him after its MOT — but tongues were beginning to wag . . .

ROY MAKES THE GOSSIP PAGES

Sandie asks Roy to attend the club's pre-season dance with her as she claims her boyfriend is away. Roy believes her every word and stupidly allows himself to be photographed with Sandie attending the dance. (Happily Roy and Penny were soon reconciled.)

THE SUPPORTERS' CLUB ARE HOLDING THEIR PRE-SEASON DANCE, NEXT WEEK, AND MY BOY-FRIEND IS AWAY ON BUSINESS! I, ER... DON'T LIKE TO WALK IN THERE...

SO YOU'VE GOT YOURSELF AN ESCORT! CONSIDER ME AS YOUR KNIGHT IN SHINING ARMOUR FOR THE EVENING!

THANKS, ROY...

CONTINUED ON BACK PAGE.

ROY of the ROVERS
CONTINUED FROM FRONT COVER

HOLD IT, ROY... WE JUST WANT A PICTURE OF YOU AND YOUR... ER ...FRIEND.

NO!

WHAT'S THE MATTER, ROY? NOT *ASHAMED* OF ME, ARE YOU?

OF COURSE NOT! IT'S JUST THAT I WOULD HAVE LIKED TO PUT THOSE PRESSMEN RIGHT ON ONE OR TWO THINGS...

EXIT

...SUCH AS YOU BEING MY SECRETARY! AND THE FACT THAT I'M ONLY ESCORTING YOU TO THIS DO, BECAUSE YOUR REGULAR BOY-FRIEND IS AWAY ON BUSINESS...

...I MEAN, WE DON'T WANT PEOPLE TO GET THE WRONG IDEA—!

OHH, FORGET THEM AND LET'S ENJOY OURSELVES! I MEAN, YOU'VE GOT ENOUGH PROBLEMS AS IT IS!

ROVERS RETURN!

MEL PARK, HOME OF MELCHESTER ROVERS, WAS THE SCENE OF THE MOST SPECTACULAR BENEFIT MATCH EVER PLAYED... AS FORMER STARS OF THE ROVERS RETURNED FOR AN HISTORIC MATCH...

Left to right: (Top) KEN COOPER, TUBBY MORTON, TERRY WEST.
(Middle) GEOFF GILES, ANDY CROYDON, PACO DIAZ, TOM DAWSON.
(Bottom) DEREK MILLAR, MERVYN WALLACE, LOFTY PEAK (Capt.), TAFFY MORGAN, JUMBO TRUDGEON.

THANKS FOR THE MEMORIES

All the old gang, a little older and fatter, turned out for a testimonial game soon after Roy made his emotional return to Melchester. A night, and a team, to remember!

with the appointment of England Test cricketer Geoff Boycott as chairman of Melchester Rovers, and ending with Roy again playing a key role in the wining of the European Cup Winners' Cup.

At the start of the next season Roy set up what he initially regarded as an exhibition match between two teams of Rovers players past and present; but the veterans 4-3 win exposed serious flaws in the younger side's game.

When Melchester started the Canon League season with a bad defeat, Roy went on a player spending spree, and bought in the 'golden oldies' Emlyn Hughes and Bob Wilson. The former scored on his debut

GUESS WHO HE'S SIGNED NOW?

Roy fully realised the commercial value of big-name celebrity signings and, as well as the Kemp brothers from Spandau Ballet, enticed former England captain Emlyn Hughes and Arsenal goalkeeper Bob Wilson to Melchester towards the end of their careers.

as Rovers beat Tynecaster. Then, Roy added a couple of London youngsters to his shopping list, Martin Kemp and Steve Norman – who were also members of new romantics pop group Spandau Ballet. Kemp made his debut in October, coming on as sub for Blackie.

With this curious mix of old, new and celebrity players, Melchester reached the Milk Cup final against Tynecaster, Bob Wilson equalling the league record of eleven straight games without conceding a goal. They turned in a poor first half performance in the final, and at half-time Roy learned the reason why. The players apparently believed that he was going to sack a lot of the older squad. Roy reassured them that it wasn't true, insisting that even if they did not want to play for him, the club or the fans, they should at least play for themselves. The verbal volley worked. Although Tynecaster scored a goal, the final whistle had been blown before the ball left the boot of the scorer, leaving Rovers the 3-0 winners and Wilson with a new record of twelve consecutive clean sheets!

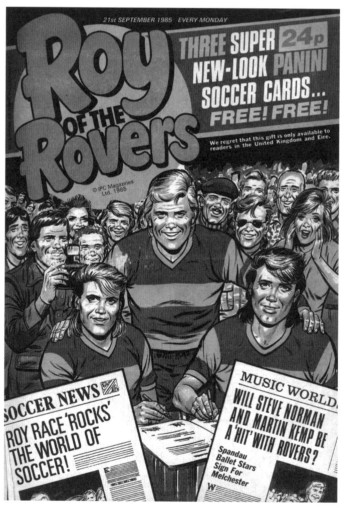

ROY RACE - SUPERFOCUS 2000

Full Name: Roy Race.

Occupation: Manager of Melchester Rovers.

Age: I decline to answer that question on the grounds that I might incriminate myself.

Your greatest achievement in life: My children.

Biggest disappointment or setback: The death of my wife Penny.

Four words that describe you: A complete football nutcase.

Who is your favourite footballer: It's still Blackie Gray.

What do you think of women's football: It's blooming. The women's World Cup in the USA was excellent.

The last sports event you paid to see: The Cricket World Cup final at Lords.

Favourite Spice Girl: Er, to be honest – No. There's one going out with a footballer, isn't there? Posh or something. Her.

You are currently reading: Last weekend's match reports.

PCs – are they for work, games, or surfing the web: Rocky's had me playing a few football games, and he usually wins. I don't think tthey're as good as table football myself.

Favourite TV programme: *Match of the Day.*

Video help on tight decisions during games – Yes or No: No. Mistakes are part of football. We all make them – players and managers seem to forget they make as many, if not more, than match officials. Yes, it's sometimes a real kick in the teeth, when you're on the wrong end of a bad decision, but usually they even themselves out over a season – as many go for you as against you.

What would you buy if you won the Lottery jackpot: A new player.

Favourite item of clothing: Whatever I'm wearing when Rovers win.

And what did it cost: Who cares as long as we win.

Who would you most like to meet: I always give the same answer, because I've still never met him. It's Pele.

How much does a loaf of bread cost: I decline to answer that on the grounds, etc., etc. ... !

Takeaways – Indian or Chinese: Er, I prefer Italian food these days.

Why answer SuperFocus questions: To give the fee to charity.

TRAGEDY - AGAIN

The following season began with Roy taking the Rovers out to Basran, to honour an earlier commitment – although some of the celebrity signings did not go on the tour, having fulfilled their contracts for the one season.

The trip would prove incident-packed and, ultimately, fatal. Harrowing enough was the kidnap attempt that the team suffered on their outward journey. But then disaster struck again when, after having been rescued, the coach collided with a car bomber resulting in the death of eight players – the same as the number of Manchester United players who perished in the Munich disaster in 1958. It was to be the saddest day in the club's proud history. The eight who died were Noel Baxter, Vic Guthrie, Trevor Cassiday, Carl Hunt, Neville Jones, Kenny Logan, Steve Naylor and Jimmy Slade.

Roy received a dislocated shoulder during the incident and was of course ruled out of the 1986 World Cup as a result. Once recovered, he shook off any despair of his own and began instead to focus on the task of rebuilding Rovers.

He brought in, among others, Mark 'Cracker' Gray (son of Blackie), and Pak Soon, a Vietnamese player who had been a boat person as a baby.

Rovers opened with a comprehensive victory over Deans Park. In October Blackie Gray returned after recovering from his injuries, and was appointed assistant manager as the club started to regen-erate. November saw Roy introducing a membership scheme to combat hooliganism, and in January Roy risked his life to avoid knocking down a young fan. In gratitude the boy's wealthy father provided Rovers with the necessary funds for the building of a family enclosure and offered a million pounds to the charity of Roy's

THE BASRAN CONNECTION TURNS SOUR

A routine pre-season trip to Basran started to go badly wrong when his team were caught up in a botched kidnap attempt. Unfortunately a much more harrowing disaster was just around the corner.

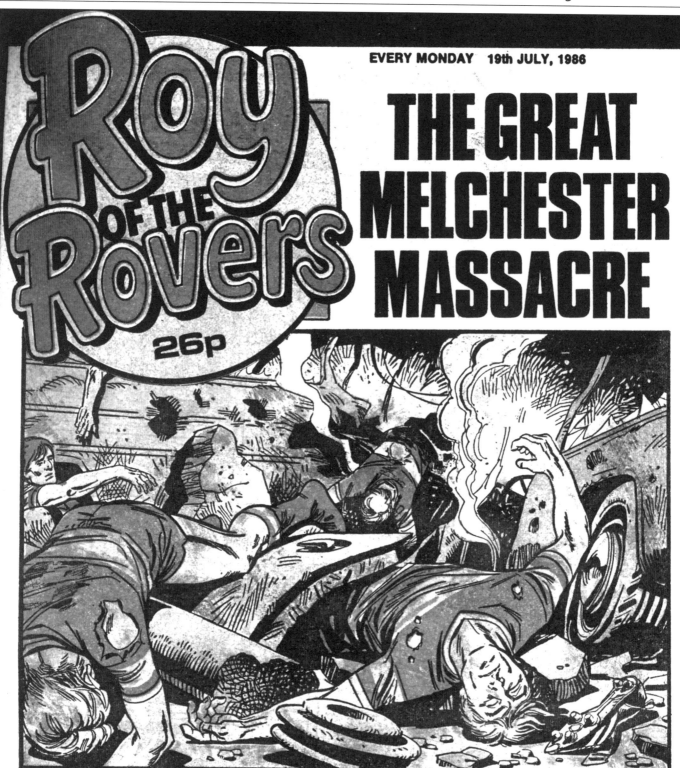

EVERY MONDAY   19th JULY, 1986

ROY OF THE ROVERS

26p

THE GREAT MELCHESTER MASSACRE

THERE is tragic news concerning mighty Melchester Rovers.
Britain's most-famous club side has been involved in tragedy, caught up in the tangled web of Basranian politics. Held captive by rebel forces, the Melchester players were rescued by an SAS unit, only to have their escape bus blown-up by an explosives-packed car driven by a rebel fanatic. The whole soccer world will be waiting for news of Roy Race and the rest of the team. Early indications are that many of the side are dead or injured. The British Embassy announced that relatives have been informed. . .

THE DAY THAT SHOCKED THE FOOTBALL WORLD
The most harrowing day in the history of Melchester Rovers. Words and pictures speak for themselves.

IT NEVER RAINS BUT POURS

Mel Park was destroyed by an 'earthquake' ten minutes into the first match of the 1988-89 season, against Blackport. Many remembered the strange ground subsidence some years earlier, and an investigation eventually revealed old, unstable mine shafts.

choice if Rovers won the Littlewood's Cup. Which, of course, they did, and Roy donated the money to the special children's unit at Melchester Hospital, while naturally dedicating the victory to those players who were killed.

The enclosure was finally opened the following season.

There was a further development in Roy's career that December when Ben Galloway suffered a minor heart attack, and Roy was promoted to General Manager. As Rovers continued to rebuild, Roy inevitably relied on a young side. Indeed, they were nicknamed the Melchester Minors. Although they lost 2-1 in the FA Cup Final to Weston Villa, they clinched the League title on the final weekend with a win over Stambridge. It was an afternoon of high emotion, the joy of victory tinged with the sadness of the circumstances.

But for all their success, life was never easy for Rovers and they could never afford to lapse into complacency. Unbelievably, yet more disaster was in store for the club.

In August 1988 an 'earthquake' destroyed Mel Park ten minutes into their first match of the season, against Blackport. Miraculously there were very few injuries among the spectators, but it seemed likely that Melchester would never play there again. It would transpire that the quake was not of natural causes: engineering works to extend the city's underground network had interfered with some old, latent mine workings beneath the stadium. The Mel Park goalposts were literally swallowed up by the chasms that formed!

Then at half time away to Portdean in the next match Rovers received an offer they could not refuse – to play at Wembley until the extensive repairs to Mel Park were complete.

Their first home match at Wembley was against Deans Park, a

2-2 draw with a last-minute penalty for Rovers after Roy was brought down. There was resentment from the London sides that Rovers had been given the honour of playing as tenants at the hallowed ground, but in fact it really left Rovers without any 'home' advantage. As a consequence, their record at the ground was poor, indeed they lost their next game 6-3.

Their poor form continued into January, but Roy set himself the challenge of becoming the first captain in the history of the FA Cup to start and finish at Wembley. They beat Third Division Selbridge Athletic in the third round at 'home', when a fracture to his right forearm forced Roy to miss the fourth round victory over Carlton Town. In the fifth round, Melchester smashed Burndean, with Roy playing as a sub, his arm in a bandage. Their League form continued to be weak, and they crashed out of the FA Cup and then had to fight against relegation, needing to ensure a win in the final game against local rivals Melborough. They emerged victorious and survived to play on in the top flight.

At the start of the 1989-90 season Roy was coming under enormous pressure from director Charlie Sutton to buy the Glenrath Celtic striker Andy Maclaren. Roy demurred, feeling that Rovers had enough strike power within the club without having to bring in expensive outsiders. But he lost the argument and Rovers broke the British transfer record by signing Maclaren for £3 million, promptly naming the expensive import as a sub in his first game, the Littlewood's Cup fourth round tie at Barndale Athletic.

Enraged at being left on the bench for his debut, when he finally took the field Maclaren responded with two goals.

Roy was still unhappy. Incorporating Maclaren into the side meant changing Melchester's style of play and adopting a 4-4-2 formation; but the system blew up in their faces in the Cup. Sutton called for Roy's resignation for failing to integrate Maclaren into the team. But Rovers soon reverted to type, and Maclaren adapted his game, even down to taking throw-ins. In February Sutton resigned as director and the new twin strike force of Roy, now in his thirty-second year as a professional footballer but looking fitter than ever, and Maclaren was quickly dubbed 'Double Dynamite'.

Rovers got through to the FA Cup final where they met Weston Villa, who beat them in the 1988 final. DJ Simon Mayo accepted the post of honorary vice president of the club. In the final, Roy put Gary Gunn – the seventeen-year-old son of his close friend and Portdean manager Richie Gunn – on the bench. Gunn's second-half shot rebounded off a post late in the game and Maclaren smashed it back in for the winner.

As English clubs re-entered Europe the following season following their ban for various acts of hooliganism, Roy warned soccer thugs that their anti-social, anti-soccer behaviour would not be tolerated. Rovers progressed to the European Cup Winners' Cup quarter finals where they suffered an unjust sending-off after an Italian player from Morino took a dive on the edge of the penalty area. The penalty was saved and Rovers went on to win the tie, only to fall in the semi-final on away goals.

Roy's son, Roy Junior, meanwhile, had been signed on schoolboy forms for Rovers in May 1991 and was immediately nicknamed 'Junior Rocky' in honour of his own very useful left-footed shot

In January the team coach was involved in another crash. Although thankfully it wasn't fatal this time, the consequences were nonetheless severe indeed. Blackie Gray was seriously injured, and had to take months out before he eventually recovered. The crash left

---

KEY 'REAL WORLD' TRANSFERS

£20,000: **1947** November: Tommy Lawton, Chelsea to Nottingham County

£65,000: **1957** May: John Charles, Leeds United to Juventus

£55,000: **1960** March: Denis Law, Huddersfield to Manchester City

£100,000: **1962** June: Denis Law, Manchester City to Torino

£11 6,000: **1962** July: Denis Law, Torino to Manchester United

£110,000: **1966** August: Alan Ball, Blackpool to Everton

£200,000: **1970** March: Martin Peters, West Ham to Spurs

£1,180,000: **1979** February: Trevor Francis, Birmingham City to Nottingham Forest

£2,000,000: **1988** July: Paul Gascoigne, Newcastle to Spurs

£2,900,000: **1991** July: Dean Saunders, Derby to Liverpool

£3,600,000: **1992** July: Alan Shearer, Southampton to Blackburn

KEY TRANSFERS IN <u>ROY OF THE ROVERS</u>

£10,000: **1955** August: Arty Hedlow, Elbury Wanderers

£85,000: **1961** August: Italian club's offer for Roy

£150,000: **1968** August: Douglas Ballard, Carford United to Melchester Rovers

£300,000: **1976** March: Duncan MacKay, Portdean City to Melchester Rovers

£700,000: **1979** May: Paco Diaz, Zaragosa to Melchester Rovers

£1,000,000: **1992** March: Nick 'Rapper' Hardisty, Railford Town to Melchester Rovers

£3,000,000: **1989** November: Andy Maclaren, Glenrath Celtic to Melchester Rovers

LIKE FATHER LIKE SON
Much to Roy's secret delight and pride his son Roy Junior – known as Junior Rocky – has proved to be an oustanding footballer in his own right. There could never be another Roy of the Rovers, but Rocky came close.

Rovers senior players severely depleted and once again Roy was forced to blood a lot of youngsters.

Being such a big name, Roy was always the target of lucrative offers from abroad, and at this juncture the mother of all carrots was dangled in front of him by the USA Soccer Federation who offered him eight million dollars over five years to prepare the USA team for the 1994 World Cup. As with the Basran connection he turned it down. Money had never been the guiding light for Roy.

The following year Rovers won the League title and added Bresden defender Karl Bruckner to the squad after being hugely impressed by him when Melchester lost to Rovers in the UEFA Cup.

As the season reached its end, Roy managed the England B team to victory in a four-nation tournament including Italy, the USA and Segovia. Rovers were now in the Premier League and their new signing Mozzie Mostin made history by scoring the first goal in the new competition.

Mostin was a bit of a clown and a show-off and his outlandish antics on the field so upset the Rovers chairman Jeremy Sinclair, that he ordered Roy to face an inquiry by the board.

Although Roy toughed it out for another six weeks, he knew that his only option was to resign, which he eventually chose to do live on Sky TV, saying that he wanted to stay on as a player, if the new manager would have him. Mervyn Wallace was promptly appointed caretaker-manager. In December Ralph 'Flash' Gordon, a former England international and manager of rival club Melboro, was appointed to the post full-time. He was instantly christened 'Ralph of the Rovers'.

Though Roy was quickly reinstated, his life was taking increasingly dramatic twists and turns, climaxing when he crashed his helicopter and ended up, for the second time in his life, critically injured and in a coma. He recovered, but only to face a startling new reality. Surgeons were left with no option but to amputate his legendary left foot.

Roy had played his last game.

He needed a complete change of scene, and after he had recovered he finally accepted an offer to coach abroad, taking charge of AC Monza. He, Penny and the girls were very happy there, while Rocky made solid progress with Melchester. But his eggshell life, still so fragile after the crash, was left in tatters in 1995 when Penny died in a car crash. The circumstances were never fully revealed, but being in Italy of course accusing fingers were pointed at the Mafia.

Roy returned to Britain seemingly a broken man and initially took an appointment with Melborough – Melchester were involved in a players' bribery scandal at the time and he initially wanted nothing to do with them. But the lure of his old team was strong, and he returned in 1997 to save them from relegation. He brought in his daughter Melinda, now a recent graduate, to look after the finances, and gradually the old ethos of the club returned – and was crowned with a splendid FA Cup win in 1999. Roy's is one of the most astonishing stories in English soccer history.

How can you ever assess such a rollercoaster career? Blackie Gray, at one stage, told the local Melchester paper that Roy was fifty per cent better than any footballer he had ever played with or against. The normal boundaries of endeavour and talent simply did not apply to him on the pitch. All things being equal Roy was untouchable. But things rarely were equal. Though a fantasy figure, when he crossed the white line onto the pitch he led a very human, realistic life and suffered the slings and arrows of outrageous fortune along with the rest of us. And there lies, it would seem, the root of his enduring appeal.

A CRUSHING BLOW
His playing career finished by the critical injuries he suffered in his helicopter crash, Roy Race was then dealt an even heavier blow with the death of his wife Penny in a suspicious car crash.

THE TEAM BEHIND THE LEGEND

As we have seen previously, Wilson of the *Wizard* and Alf Tupper were very much the creation of one man – Gilbert Dalton – whose incredible imagination and work rate sustained two of the all-time sporting comic book heroes for decades. Roy's story was much more of a team effort than that, and one man in particular, Frank Pepper, should certainly be identified as his originator.

Pepper had previously written the *Champion* series – Danny of the Dazzlers – and was asked by *Tiger* to produce a more realistic football strip. That was apparently what the readers wanted. As he recalled, 'We decided to show an ordinary lad, with talent, with whom the reader would identify, joining a top-class club with long traditions, as a very humble junior gradually making his way up the ladder, until he became a star.'

Pepper went about giving Roy the human touch – a family, a home, a regular school upbringing, friends and the occasional enemy. There was even an occasional mention of the opposite sex, which was considered fairly radical at the time. Pepper set the tone and though other commitments were such that initially he only penned the first four stories, he returned in the 1960s and 1970s to pick up and embellish the career of Roy Race.

A team of five authors, including Pepper, wrote the Roy stories and dedicated fans of the comic and the Roy strips can always tell who was responsible for what. Stewart Colwyn was in charge for four and a half years after Pepper's early efforts and was also responsible for the first, highly acclaimed, *Roy of the Rovers* annual in 1958. *Tiger's* editor Derek Birnage largely took over in 1960 and there was a brief, rather bizarre period, when the *Tiger* advertised that 'Bobby Charlton' was writing Roy's adventures – although, of course, 'Bobby Charlton' had a ghost writer, Derek Burnage himself.

Frank Pepper regularly returned the Roy stories in the 1960s and then came Tom Tully, the longest-serving of the writers who handled the helicopter crash story. Tully started writing the *Roy of the Rovers* story in 1969 and continued to do so on an intermittent basis until 1974 and then on a continuous basis until the closure of the comic in 1993. In an interview for the *Yorkshire Post* in October 1980 Tully brilliantly summed up the appeal of *Roy of the Rovers*:

The phrase 'Roy of the Rovers' should be in the dictionary. Roy represents something that coloured your life when you were young. He has become something people relate to and use to express themselves. He makes mistakes, feels guilty, loses his temper, makes errors of judgement, has arguments with his wife and frequently finishes up with egg on his face. But in the final analysis he is thoroughly decent, totally loyal and widely respected.

Finally came Ian Rimmer who, having contributed a number of stories in the autumn of 1993, provided the last ever scripts for the story, which appeared in the monthly BBC *Match of the Day* magazine until it ceased publication in May 2001.

Sharing the glory and an equal billing with the writers must be the artists who brought the character to life with such skill and humour for over forty years. The first we have already met, though under a different name. When Frank Pepper stood down it was the existing artist Joe Colquhoun who took over the scripting – in the name of Stewart Colwyn!

Then came Paul Trevillion, one of Europe's finest sports artists, who also made a mark with his illustrations of golf, basketball and American football. 'I always felt the weight of Roy's many fans who expected so much from the artwork. It is a stage in my career I look back on with a great deal of affection.'

Yvonne Hutton took over in 1968, as Trevillion's interests started to broaden out. Hutton started drawing Roy in the 1967-68 period and she was also the first artist to draw the *Roy of the Rovers* story when it appeared in the *Daily Star*. It was during this period that Yvonne was tragically killed in a car accident.

David Sque drew the *Roy of the Rovers* story from January 1975 to August 1986. He gave Roy a new image, and he became famous for the flowing blond locks he sported during this period. Many believe the lead singer of the band Sweet was the model. David was the Roy artist at the time of the launch of the *Roy of the Rovers* comic in 1976.

Although not a fanatical supporter of football, this was never evident in David's fine detailed work which he produced from his home in Swanage, Dorset. Apparently he took four full days to draw and colour both pages of artwork. Mondays were taken up with sketching the first page and on Tuesday the second page was sketched. Wednesday was the brush and Indian ink stage and Thursday was usually the day when David would apply the colour, starting with the larger areas and moving to the more intricate work, finishing the sky, the stands and the crowd first and then concentrating on the players. Both pages were completed by Thursday night.

Mike White drew the *Roy of the Rovers* story from August 1986 to October 1992. Mike gave Roy a more powerful, muscular look. One of Mike's most popular covers was the one for the book *Roy of the Rovers – The Playing Years*. In June 1999 he designed one of the four new Royal Mail Millennium stamps – he was responsible for the 26p first class stamp, number twenty-seven, which celebrates England's World Cup win in 1966.

Finally Barrie Mitchell first drew the *Roy of the Rovers* story in October 1992 and was the artist at the time of the closure of the comic in March 1993. He was also the artist chosen to resurrect him in 1997.

THEY ALSO SERVED

We have covered fully the lives of the titans: the three longest-lived, best-loved, and most truly prodigious and fantastic of the comic-book heroes. But each comic in which they appeared featured half a dozen other heroes – some war heroes like Braddock VC, others sportsmen themselves. And over the many decades that Wilson, Tough of the Track and Roy Race were playing and competing – the span, indeed, of several complete sporting careers for a mere mortal – new comics came and went, times and society changed, and the supporting cast of characters evolved and changed too. Here are the best of the rest.

One of the most popular – a huge favourite, not to mention a huge man – was Johnny Cougar, who should not be confused with the Bruce Springsteen-sound-alike singer of the Eighties who had a top 10 hit with 'Jack and Diane'. As regular readers of *Tiger* will recall, Johnny Cougar was a ferocious, full-blown Seminole Red Indian matman (wrestler to you and me) from Canada who, along with his agent and manager, Bill MacLean – a distinctly dodgy character – travelled the world taking on all-comers, in and out of the ring. As well as defeating every human in sight he overcame various members of the animal kingdom, notably Bear, Tiger, Bull and Wolf and, in true Wilson style, even found himself competing in, and winning, an international decathlon.

Television wrestling today is bracketed with pantomime and vaudeville, but throughout the Sixties and Seventies, strange to relate, it was treated as a serious sport and

JOHNNY COUGAR – MATMAN EXTRAORDINAIRE!
Above all else Johnny Cougar, the Seminole Red Indian wrestler, was a magnificent athlete never matched for strength in or out of the ring. Original drawings of the various comic strips by Sandy James are much prized by comic collectors.

YET ANOTHER TROPHY FOR JOHNNY

Later in his career he teamed up with 'Splash Gorton', who was clearly Frank Zappa's twin bother. Splash was always described as a 'Beatnik', a term that would go unrecognised by the youth of today.

attracted huge audiences on Saturday afternoons. ITV executives used to put it up against the best that the BBC's *Grandstand* had to offer – including Five Nations rugby, Test cricket and Wimbledon – and still win the ratings war. Commentator Kent Walton became one of the best-known voices on TV, while competitors such as Jackie Pallo, Mick McManus and the Royal brothers, a dynamic tag team, were household names. Given professional wrestling's rather tenuous grip on reality, it was not long before life started imitating art, with the appearance of Apache War Cloud, to be followed by other 'characters' such as Billy Two-Rivers and the Mohawk from Caughnawaga. Perhaps anything was possible by the time of Ricki Starr, a former ballet dancer from Missouri went into action in the ring wearing ballet pumps.

Johnny Cougar himself was an upstanding character who always tried to fight fairly, but in one contest against "Pretty Boy" Baker he became so disillusioned by all the cheating that he threw away the rulebook and even stamped on the guy's face, before turning his attention to the crooked McLean, whom he should really have dumped years earlier.

Much of the attraction of the Cougar stories came from the brilliant line drawings of the late Sandy James, who was generally considered the best in the business. His action pictures are remarkably full of life, with muscle and sinew straining in perfect unison, and his storyboards are much sought after by collectors. Nobody could quite draw a taught bicep or straining quadracep like James.

Another *Tiger* stalwart was the dashing Formula 1 World Champion Skid Solo, who should not be confused with Napoleon of *The Man From U.N.C.L.E.* fame. Skid Solo was a daredevil racer who was equally proficent in a rally car or astride a powerful motorbike, indeed anything with wheels. It might be surprising to some that Formula One could spawn a comic book sports hero, but remember that the Sixties and Seventies were the halcyon days of British motor racing heroes like Jackie Stewart, Jim Clark, John Surtees and James Hunt. Johnny Cougar was perhaps the exception that proved the rule: the key ingredient for a comic book sporting hero was a real-life Briton reigning supreme.

Skid claimed his fair share of front pages with his exploits, and his incredible driving skills were often needed to outwit the various villains and hoodlums that seemed to populate the world of motor sport. A spice of reality was added to the fantasy fun with *Tiger*'s reproduction of accurate circuit diagrams of all the famous real-life tracks where Skid raced, with all the corners and straights named – a practice subsequently taken up by many of the news-papers when reporting actual Grands Prix.

Throughout everything he was loyally supported by his

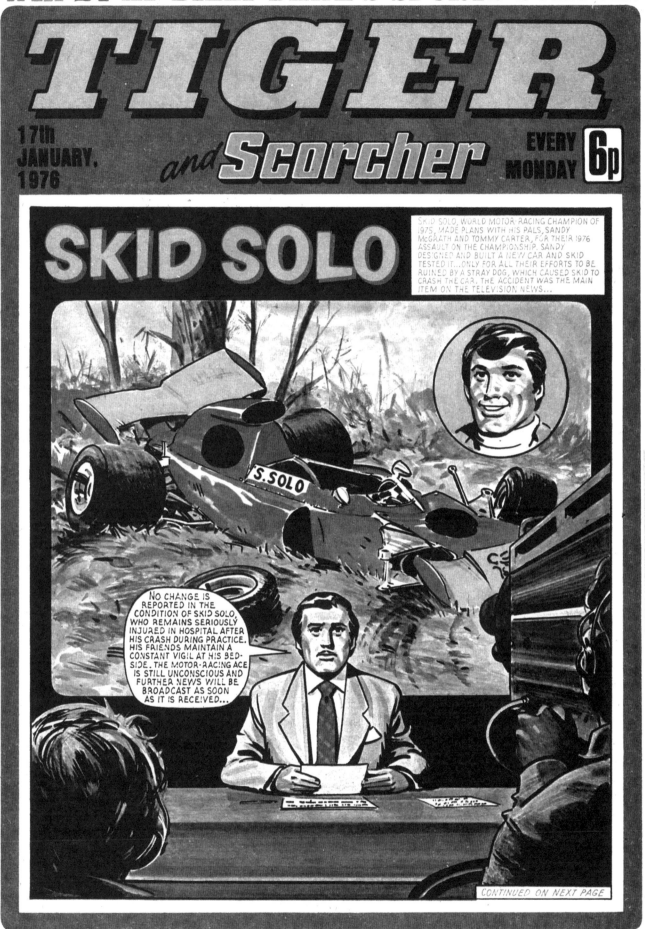

chief mechanic, Sandy McGrath, and his mustard-keen trainee, Sparrow Smith. Chief Mechanic does scant justice to McGrath, the archetypal gritty Scot in dirty overalls, who was so much more than a grease monkey. Indeed, at one stage he even took on the mantle of Chief Designer, and drew up plans for the fastest car Skid had ever driven. But the project was sadly frustrated when a dog ran out onto the circuit during practice one day, Skid crashed at a tad under 200mph, and ended up in hospital and out of the sport for a season.

Skid is probably best remembered though for his shocking exit from the *Tiger*. Firstly, his best mate was killed during a race – all the action was graphically drawn – and for the next couple of weeks a devastated Skid started seeing his ghost by the track. Then, as he practised for the last big Grand Prix of the season, Skid saw the ghost waving frantically at him. It was a premonition which heralded the worst crash of Skid's life. He bravely fought off death but was apparently left so badly disfigured that, for the last couple of weeks of the story, the reader was never allowed to see his ravaged face, and eventually Skid Solo was pushed off into the sunset in a wheelchair.

Harsh stuff, but the reality of F1 at the time was the high number of fatalities and *Tiger* felt compelled to try to reflect that reality. It has to be said, however, that there is another theory about the ending of that story: namely, that the *Tiger* artist who drew the strip quit one day in a drunken fury, and the house artist called in at short notice to deputise just couldn't do Skid.

Another *Tiger* favourite was Hotshot Hamish, the gentle

SKID WOULD SCRAP FOR EVERY POINT
One of the great sporting tragedies is that we never got to hear Murray Walker and James Hunt commentating on a Skid Solo drive. A match made in heaven, surely.

giant from the Outer Hebrides who could kick a ball like no other man on earth. A former caber-tosser, Hamish was brought from a tiny island to play for Scottish League club Princes Park by manager Mr McWhacker. While at Park, Hamish formed a devastating, if eccentric, partnership with Kevin 'Mighty' Mouse, and together they helped Park win

the Scottish Cup. He also owned, as you do, a pet sheep called McMutton. There was, as you can see, no stereotyping in this series at all. Sartorially Hamish left a little to be desired, and spent much of his time wearing the biggest, baggiest, jumper in the world which had been knitted by his ageing grandmother back home.

Tiger around this era spawned many of the more unlikely characters in boys' comics. Redstone Rovers toured Australia one pre-season and suffered a calamitous injury to their England centre forward 'Striker' Short, who broke a leg. On the way back to the airport, the Redstone team had stopped for an impromptu kick around when the captain spotted something in the distance. It was a herd of kangaroos, being chased by a jeep, which was trying and capture them, and running among the kangaroos was a boy. Suddenly the boy

came across a loose football and launched it like a rocket at the driver of the jeep, who was knocked clean out of his seat with the impact. 'No goalie in the world could keep a ball from him out of the net!', marvelled one of the team. 'There's our replacement for Striker Short!' enthused another. And the Kangaroo Kid, no sooner said than done, was brought to Britain where he became a football star.

Billy's Boots – the adventures of Billy Dane – was another big favourite with readers, with the story of the rather ordinary fourth-former who was absolutely useless at football and always got picked last in playground kickarounds being transformed into a world beater. Billy made his debut in 1970 in *Scorcher*, moved to *Tiger* in 1974, made a brief appearance in *Eagle* in 1985 and played out his days in the *Roy of the Rovers* comic from 1986.

ANOTHER HOTSHOT FROM HAMISH!
He was unstoppable
Trained as a caber tosser and nurtured on porridge oats on a remote island in the Western Isles, Hotshot Hamish turned to football with devastating effect after Princes Park manager Mr Mcwhacker spotted his incredible talent.

ALONE THE KID BEGAN THE DESPERATE SEARCH FOR HIS KANGAROO FRIENDS!

KANGAROO KID

Decades before Australia became a footballing power, Redstone Rovers stumbled across the incredible 'Kangaroo Kid' during a pre-season tour 'down under'.

BILLY'S BOOTS

Billy Dane found the battered old football boots of Dead Shot Keen and then subsequently met the retired hero himself. But his ability to play like Dead Shot whenever he wore them was always threatened by his gran's determination to throw them away…

It was Billy Dane's good fortune to be rummaging away in his grandmother's attic one day, as is often the case with our comic book heroes he seems to be a bit of a stray, with no mention of parents, when he unearthed a pair of football boots, ancient but in good order. He also came across an air rifle, but fortunately it was the boots that took his fancy). They had belonged to the legendary former England centre-forward 'Dead Shot' Keen, a hero of his grandfather's, who had taken the opportunity to acquire the boots as a memento.

Billy did what any inquisitive schoolboy would do, and put the boots on for a kickabout. The results were dramatic. As if by magic the boots made Billy move every time to the right position on the pitch, and suddenly the school nerd was scoring sensational goals and winning big finals for his side. Within months he was scoring goals for the England Schools. This then set up a predictable trajectory for most of the strip's subsequent storylines: on the eve of a big match Billy loses his boots. On one occasion his granny kindly donated them to a jumble sale collection; on another she put them in the dustbin. But without fail, thankfully, Billy would find them again just in the nick of time.

And, would you believe it, Billy also discovered a pair of Keen's cricket boots? 'Dead Shot' Keen turned out to have been an England Test cricketer as well, and this battered footwear proved to have a comparable effects on Billy's performance on the cricket field during the summer months. So occasionally lightning does strike twice.

One of my own all-time favourite strips was Lags X1, about the Bankhurst Prison football team, which borrowed shamelessly from the Peter Sellers film *Two-Way Stretch*, with several of the major cartoon characters bearing an uncanny resemblance to its stars: Lionel Jeffries, Bernard Cribbins and the great Sellers himself. Willie Smith, known universally as Brilliant Genius, is clearly the Sellers character Dodger, right down to the distinctive glasses, while the Chief Prison officer, 'Bad News' Benson, looks like, stands like and even shouts like CPO Sidney 'Sour' Crout, the marvellous Lionel Jeffries character. Even the storylines of this extremely amusing strip sometimes borrowed heavily from the original film: in one, Brilliant Genius effortlessly breaks out of prison to frame 'Orace Oskins, the dynamic centre forward and villain, for a crime he didn't commit, so that 'Orace can be locked up in jail himself just in time to appear for Lags 11 in their big match against Cloggin Albion. Showing selfless team spirit, Brilliant Genius then breaks back into the prison in order to be able to mastermind their successful Cup run.

Philip Driver, another singular comic hero, was, unsurprisingly, a professional golfer who was accompanied around the world by his trusty caddie Peanut Jones. Driver shared with his real-life counterparts a partiality for traditionally garish roll-neck sweaters, but what the world at large didn't know, and where the similarity ends, is that his and Peanuts' sporting occupations provided the perfect cover for them to double as crack agents for MI5. Then again, I always

MISSION ACCOMPLISHED, BRILLIANT GENIUS BROKE BACK INTO BANKHURST PRISON!

LAGS ELEVEN

Willie Smith, aka 'Brilliant Genius', bore an uncanny resemblance to the Peter Sellers character Dodger in the film Two Way Stretch. Prison warder 'Bad News Benson' was clearly modelled on Sidney 'Sour' Crout, the marvellous prison officer played by Lionel Jeffries. Some of the storylines had a familiar ring as well.

"DON'T CALL ME BAD-NEWS, YOU MUTINOUS, ILL-MANNERED TWIT!"

thought Nick Faldo had a hint of James Bond about him.

One Philip Driver storyline that stays in the mind was of the time when, out on the course during the Mulvaney Championship on the west coast of Ireland, he was the subject of an assassination attempt by Mitsumu, a dastardly Japanese who dealt in black-market diamonds. As Mitsumu's bullet whistled past his shoulder, Driver spotted a 'golfer' running along the skyline some 250 yards away pulling a trolley and toting something that looked more like a rifle than a driver. Philip immediately dropped a ball onto the fairway, took out a two-iron and cracked the shot of his life to knock the would-be assassin out cold. Even Tom Watson at his best would have been proud of that iron shot.

In the sixties, with the likes of the late Tommy Simpson winning the world road race championship and flying the flag for Britain in the Tour de France, the popularity of road cycling was reflected in a cartoon series called, with stunning originality, 'The Yellow Jersey'. It featured the extraordinary exploits of one Tearaway Tetford, who came

from nowhere to win the Tour of Britain, without even the support of a team.

Tearaway has to be considered a little dodgy, though: periodically he would disappear into his 'oily' manager's van and come out a rejuvenated figure who rode like the wind. Perhaps he was 'firing up', as the old cyclists called the rather crude habit of taking amphetamines. Or perhaps he was just indulging in yoga-style mantras – top British rider Jack Jenkins stumbled across him one night repeating over and over again, 'You will win, you will win, nothing can beat you.' A man of mystery, then, and thus he must remain until I stumble across the copies of *Rover* I'm missing from around 1970 to discover whether he was successful when he entered the Tour de France.

By way of an antidote to the Tough of the Track, the *Rover* conceived of a diametrically opposed character, the Blue Streak, who first appeared in 1960. Piers Mornington was the so called 'Toff of the Track', whose father was a famous rowing Blue and brother college captain of cricket.

THE CROWD ROARED WITH APPROVAL AS THE LONE GIPSY BOY BORE DOWN ON THE SHAKEN SCRANTHORPE DEFENCE!

Highboro' United—a lowly First Division club that once had been world-famous—was on the brink of disaster owing to the old-fashioned outlook of its directors. However, manager Baldy Hagan was convinced that he had found a future star in a strange gipsy boy named Raven, so he played the lad against Scranthorpe Athletic without consulting the club chairman. Thanks to Raven, United were soon on top, and the young gipsy had just scored his second goal, to make the score 3–0, when Sir Mortimer Child-Beale, the chairman, arrived...

RAVEN ON THE WING

Raven, the young gipsy boy, was something of a mystery, and possessed almost mystical powers on the wing. Playing barefoot, he showed uncanny anticipation and remarkable strength for one so young.

Piers then turned up at St Michael's College Cambridge to take the athletics world by storm with a minimum of effort, proving to be a sprinter of world class. The dialogue in these stories was superbly authentic and nearly 50 years later still reads well. Though talented and not a 'bad 'un' as such, Piers predictably struggled to equal Alf Tupper's popularity and soon disappeared from the scene. Gone but not forgotten.

While we're on the subject of toffs, there is also Gorgeous Gus. He was an absolute belter, an aristocrat with incalculable wealth who was so disgusted by the performance of his favourite football club, Redburn Rovers, that he bought them up lock, stock and barrel one afternoon and then enticed six of England's top players to join overnight. The news of these amazing signings was delivered to the club by Gus's butler Mr Jenkins, who always referred to his boss as the Master. There was one condition, however, which puzzled manager Sam Hopkins: one space on the teamsheet

The Marvels are all set to become the fittest team in the country—if they can survive the Colonel's new kind of Commando course for footballers!

The MUDTOWN MARVELS

MUDTOWN ATHLETIC, better known as "The Muddlers" or "The Marvels", having reached the third round of the F.A. Cup for the first time in their history, were drawn against Woolhampton Wanderers, leaders of the First Division. Even the Marvels' most fervent supporters gave them little chance of success—except, of course, Colonel Montgomery-Gore, to whom defeat, being unacceptable, was unthinkable. Accordingly, he approached the club with a revolutionary plan of attack.

DISCIPLINE AND STRATEGY ARE WHAT WE NEED, GENTLEMEN. I'VE TOLD YOU MY PLAN—NOW IT'S UP TO YOU.

THE COLONEL'S SCHEME WILL MAKE THEM AS HARD AS NAILS, JACK. I'M ALL FOR IT.

The new training programme started that same evening.

GO AHEAD, COLONEL, THEY'RE ALL YOURS!

NOW, I PUT CASEY OVER THIS COURSE THIS AFTERNOON. HE'S GOING TO SHOW YOU WHAT TO DO WHILE I GIVE A RUNNING COMMENTARY. DOUBLE AWAY, LAD.

DRIBBLE TOWARDS THE WALL AND SHOOT FOR THE CIRCLE AS SOON AS YOU'RE THROUGH THE POSTS.....

CHIP OVER THE WALL AND GO AFTER IT!

THE MUDTOWN MARVELS

Colonel Montgomery-Gore set about sharpening up the Mudtown Marvels for their big Cup match by sending them on a commando course. Footballs were provided, of course.

was to be left free for the derby game at the weekend against Redburn city.

That, of course, was to be filled by Gorgeous Gus, who took the field (after all the plebs had already run out) from his own specially erected tented pavilion, attended by Jenkins and wearing a smoking jacket over his kit. The crowd scoffed, but not for long: Gorgeous Gus could kick the ball almost as hard as Hotshot Hamish and blasted a spectacular hat-trick before retiring – this in the days before substitutes, and in the manner of a batsman 'retiring' after cracking a double century. Gorgeous Gus was well ahead of his time, in many ways the forerunner of some of the rich clowns who have subsequently become involved with football. Unlike them, however, he was good enough to contribute on the pitch as well.

Another perennial favourite was footballer Limpalong

Leslie in the *Wizard*. An orphan, lame from a childhood accident, he did not seem to have much going for him. Nonetheless, he demonstrated a work ethic to put most teenagers of his day, let alone the present time, to shame, and the handicap of having a left leg shorter than his right diminished his dedication to soccer not one bit. He practised every moment he had free from his shepherding duties on his uncle and aunt's farm, developing a mesmerising body swerve and a deadly kick, as well as an ability to trap a ball from any angle at any height.

Perseverance was the message that ran through Limpalong Leslie's professional and sporting life. Readers quickly appreciated that Limpalong Leslie was someone special, and he ranked just behind Wilson and Braddock VC in their affections. He had two main ambitions: one, to train a champion trials sheepdog – he was no mug as a dog

GORGEOUS GUS

Gorgeous Gus in all his pomp! - a born aristocrat but a magnificent footballer. Fans soon referred to him simply as 'The Master'.

handler and shepherd and demonstrated a keen eye for stock at various livestock markets; the other was to play for Darbury Rangers, the club his father John, a former England international, played for for many years. John, before his untimely death along with Leslie's mother in a car crash, had also been a two-time winner of an international sheepdog trial with a dog called Skipper, so Limp Along was clearly trying to emulate his hero figure of a father. Indeed, Limpalong Leslie – full name Leslie Tomson – was so far from your conventional sporting hero that his main profession, strictly speaking, was farming. Farming came first, soccer second, as he insisted on playing as a part-time professional so that he could fulfil his duties on the farm.

After several years of knock-backs he did eventually ended up playing for Darbury Rangers, but only by circuitous route to success. He began with non-league Peak Town, moved on to Minsterton, before joining Rockstone Athletic, a feeder club to Darbury, before finally joining the First Division club. Along the way he made various influential friends and allies, from Ishmael the genius gypsy footballer who never needed to train, and the Revd Robert Rawson, an Oxford Blue at soccer and an old team-mate of

his father's, to Eli Evans, an eccentric hill farmer. Limpalong learnt a little from them all. There were plenty of adventures along the way: sheep stealers to be thwarted; a mystery man to track down after his pack of dogs had been killing sheep at night and terrorising the neighbourhood – even the kidnap of Limpalong's demon trial-winning dog Pal. The strength of the bond between man and dog was demonstrated in another story when Pal had one of his legs broken by rival drovers and Limpalong sold one of his father's Cup Winner's medals to pay the vet's bill. The dog also ended up with a limp but, like his owner, overcame that handicap to achieve great things.

The list is by no means exhausted, but there we must leave it. Ridiculous, fantastic, unlikely, humorous, entertaining, escapist: our comic book heroes were many things to many people, but the common theme that unites them is that they were all winners. They were also essentially good people, perhaps tending a little towards blandness in their later incarnations. Certainly as the years went on the storylines and artwork never seemed to quite reach the exacting standards set in the immediate post-war decades. But they were still wonderful value for money, and once the overt nationalism, and even on occasion an undeniable racism, had been eradicated – the comics' stories had in fairness only been reflecting the society of the time – their heroes were a huge moral force for good. Nothing since has fully replaced them. To witness an eight- or nine-year-old picking up an old annual today and losing himself in it suggests that the genre may yet reappear. A good story is always a good story, and a hero is always a hero.